HOW TO LIVE TO BE 22

KEITH WATERHOUSE

HOW TO LIVE TO BE 22

THE BRITISH LIBRARY

First published in 2013 by
The British Library
96 Euston Road
London NW1 2DB

© 2013 The Estate of Keith Waterhouse
Preface © 2013 Michael Parkinson

British Library Cataloguing-in-Publication Data
A catalogue record for this book is available from The British Library

ISBN 978 0 7123 0969 1

Designed and typeset in Monotype Joanna by illuminati, Grosmont
Printed in Great Britain by MPG Printgroup

CONTENTS

PREFACE

MICHAEL PARKINSON

Keith Waterhouse always claimed he was a lazy man. This from someone who wrote sixty books, television series, West End plays, screenplays, including *Whistle Down the Wind* and Alfred Hitchcock's *Torn Curtain* – not to mention the millions of words he wrote as a columnist for the *Daily Mirror* and the *Daily Mail* from 1970 to 2009. During these years he defined the columnist's art.

He was a peppery social commentator, irascible without ever losing his sense of humour. He both satirised and immortalised the Councillors of Clogthorpe and Sharon and Tracy, who became National Institutions as they gave Essex Girls' view of the world we live in.

Then there was 'The Association for the Annihilation of the Aberrant Apostrophe', and the Eurofatcats, Messrs Waffle (Belgium), Pommefrite (France), Mortadella (Italy), Fruitcake (UK), Sardine (Portugal), and never forgetting Herr Bratwurst of Germany.

He also found time to write one of the great comic novels – *Billy Liar* – and a comedy masterpiece for the stage and Peter O'Toole: *Jeffrey Bernard Is Unwell*. His long partnership with Willis Hall was equally prolific.

I first met Keith through my friendship with Willis. In the late 1960s he invited me to their office in Shaftesbury Avenue where they were working on a play. When I arrived they were both sitting at desks staring at a wall chart which depicted – I guessed – the storyline for their work.

I sat quietly awaiting a demonstration of the collaborators' creative process. After about half an hour, when nothing moved and the only sound I heard was a pencil being taken from a pot and then being replaced, Keith looked at Willis and said: 'Well, that should do it' and we left for a long lunch during which we talked of many things except how to write a play together. Their working method was once described by the journalist Mike Molloy as 'verging on the telepathic' and I cannot think of a more precise description.

Lunch was an important part of Keith's day. He belonged to the carousing, bibulous generation of hacks who regarded Fleet Street drinking establishments as branch offices and spent a great deal of time and money yarning, arguing, debating and sometimes brawling until turning-out time when the only certainty was that next day you'd feel crapulent. All except Keith Waterhouse.

No matter how much he drank the night before he turned up the next day fit and able to write with his customary wit and precision. He explained that God had blessed him with the gift of 'the delayed hangover' which meant he only felt crapulous after he had finished his work.

Few journalists have been so admired by fellow hacks as Keith Waterhouse. Truth be told we envied him, his flowing style, his wit, his industry and above all the seeming non-chalant ease with which he produced works of unblemished quality. Those of us who gathered at St Paul's Church, Covent Garden in March 2010 to celebrate his life could not have imagined that, for all the tributes and fine speeches, he would have the last word.

He left behind an unpublished book he wrote in 1951 when he was twenty-two, married and working on the Yorkshire Evening Post in Leeds, at the very beginning of his career. It is called *How to Live to Be 22* and it contains the dreams, doubts, desires, ambitions of a young man trying to make sense of growing into adulthood.

He says in his introduction: 'I have written it for the same reason that any young man of twenty-two writes a book, because I am in a sustained coma of industrious exuberance of having got a good idea, because my friends are going to wish that they had thought of it first and because many people are going to pay me a great many compliments about it. This is not being conceited; this is being a twenty-two year old.'

If he was that confident, why wasn't the book published? Maybe, after getting it off his chest and reading it back, he came to the conclusion it was too much of a torrent of ideas and opinions, sometimes bordering on a rant. And he might have been right. Except, emerging as it has four years after the death of Keith Waterhouse, it offers a fascinating insight into the DNA of a gifted writer and where and how his ideas and opinions were formed.

For instance he always insisted that Billy Liar, the account of a daydreaming young lad in a North Country town, was not based on himself. And yet the young Waterhouse, born into a tough working-class background on a council estate near Leeds tells us of joining the Young Conservatives when he was seventeen and sauntering into the Conservative Club 'being condescending to the porter and wondering if he thought I was rich. I got the same feeling as I had as a child when I would put on a limp to make people believe I had a broken leg.'

At the same time he raised from the dead his greengrocer father and made him captain of a destroyer. Or else he claimed he sold fruit from a barrow, became bankrupt and died of undernourishment.

The young Mr Waterhouse also denied his secondary school education in favour of an impoverished lad who left school at fourteen and worked in a string factory, a cobbler's shop, a coffin makers and as a garage hand, rent collector, newspaper boy and ice cream vendor. Moreover he would tell of his oldest brother playing trumpet in the street for pennies after returning wounded in the First World War and being unable to find work.

He imagined himself going to war when seven thousand marched and only four returned. 'And in the victory parade we four limped with our flag at half mast ... and they played the Death March for us and instead of cheering ... the people took off their hats to us and stood in silence as we marched proudly by, one of us in a bath chair, me with my arm in a sling.'

As you read his fantasy you can hear Billy Liar's dad saying 'Our Billy's bloody daft, that's what he is.'

Summing up Billy, Waterhouse writes: 'I thought so often and for so long about poverty, searching for new and entertaining stories, that often a lump would come in my throat and I would actually believe I was as poor as a church mouse.'

Keith Waterhouse confesses to having spent eight of his twenty-two years 'in daydreaming luxurious extravagant concoctions that might be escapism or wishful thinking, or what, I don't know.' In fact the daydreams became his career and his life. In the book he tells of meeting a friend called Walsh on a daily basis and forming a society against those who ended a sentence with a preposition or split an infinitive. He thought he was being pedantic. Maybe, but he was also paving the way for his war on the aberrant apostrophe.

He says 'one day I want to be a columnist' and in preparation he invents a paper in which he writes 'a Daily Mirror Cassandra Column' – wishful thinking shortly to be made real. He says he wants to be a good reporter and quotes Quentin Reynolds, the great American journalist, who summed up his craft thus: 'I belong to a good profession, a profession begun by a few excellent reporters named Matthew, Mark, Luke and John. Some great reporter in Genesis told the story of the world in 400 words and there are only 297 words in the Ten Commandments. That is great reporting.'

He wonders how the book will look. Will it have a yellow cover? How it will be received? 'Will the Sunday Pictorial attack it ... will I see it in Smith's bookshop?' What will his teachers think?

In the end, for whatever reason, the book was never published until now. And now, knowing what we do about the author, it becomes a fascinating insight into the dreams and ambitions of a truly talented writer.

When he was alive Keith Waterhouse did not like talking about himself. He rarely gave interviews – and when he did always gave the impression of wishing he was somewhere else. We, who admired and loved him, were eager for explanation of how the chrysalis became the butterfly. We never heard the answers. Until now.

INTRODUCTION

ROBERT WATERHOUSE

'I had turned out a successful radio play and a few bits and pieces for magazines,' wrote my father in *Streets Ahead* (1995), the sequel to his memoir *City Lights* (1994):

> I had written an unpublished (and unpublishable) volume of autobiography called *How to Live to Be 22*, a bid at clipping three years off the record set by Beverly Nichols with his precocious memoirs *Twenty Five*. But I was not really getting anywhere...

Little did he know.

My father published two volumes of memoirs during his lifetime and was researching another, to be titled *Mother's Day*, when he died at the age of eighty in his flat in Earl's Court, London. *How to Live to Be 22* might conceivably be called volume 1a, or volume i, as it is an unashamedly unrevised memoir of 'Youth', written by my father in 1951, shortly after he had settled down with my mother in Leeds. It is a restless, impatient book, the literary equivalent of jangling change in one's pocket, and it marks the point at which my father, having fulfilled his determination to be a reporter ('another cat show loomed,' he later wrote of his immediate journalistic prospects), is anxious to become a famous writer of books and 'one day ... a columnist' like Cassandra of the *Daily Mirror* – an ambition he realized twenty years later.

It was while sorting my father's papers after his death that we – my sister Sarah, my father's longtime companion Stella Bingham, and I – came across the manuscript, although it would be more accurate to say that the manuscript passed through our hands as we chucked it into a cardboard box. This requires some explanation. My father was a magpie when it came to papers, hoarding, in dusty cupboards and drawers, skyscrapers of periodicals and ancient, yellowing receipts on which the figures had long been rendered in-visible by age, and our task was the Sisyphean one of going through the results of a lifetime spent at the typewriter. Our goal was to sort the notes, drafts, false starts, abandoned ideas and ephemera which, alone, would give anyone considering taking up writing for a living considerable pause, and divide them between two mountainous sets of boxes.

The first set, which my father's will left to the University of Cardiff, contained his journalism: not only thousands of columns but early clippings, dating back to his days as a reporter on the *Yorkshire Evening Post* and the *Daily Mirror*, and correspondence pertaining to sixty odd years in newspapers (including letters, often the fodder for columns, documenting glorious rows with cowering representatives of borough councils, the Post Office, and British Rail).

The second mountain might be called Almost Everything Else of Literary Interest – film and TV scripts, realized or abandoned; play scripts; manuscripts; and letters to and from collaborators, actors, directors, teachers, and students (though he grumbled about questionnaires from students who hadn't read his work, and who were hoping that he'd do their class projects for them, my father tried to answer all such queries). It was in this set that we'd mercifully managed – as they had more room than us – to interest the British Library. It included the shooting script for *Torn Curtain*, which my father and Willis wrote (uncredited) for Alfred Hitchcock, to which was attached the director's characteristically formal and extensive notes (the characters played by 'Mr. Newman and Ms. Andrews,' Hitchcock advised, might both satisfy the Hollywood Code and convey a sexual relationship simply by appearing, dressed, in a hotel bedroom together); and letters to young, would-be authors, to whom my father usually offered the advice 'write something, anything, every day,' but who, if they'd cast their eyes upon the number of rejected or abandoned manuscripts this mountain of papers included, might have queasily chosen another profession.

There was also a third, more tentative collection, the Not Sure If We Should Part With This pile. Some manuscripts, such as those dating from his long collaboration with Willis

Hall, for example, found a logical home with the Hall family; still others we felt we should pass on to my father's surviving relatives and friends; books that were of great value to my father we kept. The Not Sure If... pile contained the second draft of *Billy Liar* (he left the first, which he later described as 'pretentious', in a taxi), which the British Library has now made available to readers in a digital version; annotated copies of *A Kind of Loving*, which he and Willis adapted for the screen, and Jeffrey Bernard's signed collection of *Low Life* columns, which became the material for *Jeffrey Bernard Is Unwell*; entire bookcases of research on Leeds and Soho, subjects to which he often and lovingly returned, and which included ongoing research his niece had kindly gathered for him for *Mother's Day*; thick scrapbooks of research he and Willis Hall put together, among them ideas for a film based on the First World War; and the collected antics of their invention, Vernon Laxton, the centre of an elaborate, long-running practical joke that Willis and my father played, in the 1960s, on agents, producers, editors, and other writers, whom they tormented with letters enclosing brief samples of a play in verse and attempts to solicit interest in a three-hour rock opera about the patron saint of cobblers.

By the time all the boxes were full, they took up most of the floor of a spare room and teetered towards the ceiling. It was a humbling sight.

My father's study, which I regarded as more or less off-limits while he lived, was especially treacherous. Besides dusty hillocks of files, reference books, and maps, it housed his several typewriters, the most impressive of which has now joined the Garrick Club, and his extensive collection of newspaper memorabilia, which, thanks to *The Daily Mail* and Bill Hagerty, the former Chairman of the Journalists' Charity and former editor of *The People* and *British Journalism Review*, is now the centrepiece of the Keith Waterhouse Library at the Charity's nursing home for retired and distressed journalists. (It is also home to two cats, which would make my father happy.)

His study also contained a metal trunk that held, for my sister Sarah and me, the most extraordinary collection of all. Though he could be an expansive and extravagant father who was proud of all three of his children (our elder sister, Penny, died in 1998), he retained a Northerner's reserve when it came to private matters, and outwardly could be as unsentimental as he was notoriously intolerant (in his eulogy at the Memorial Service at St Paul's, Covent Garden, Sir Michael Parkinson noted that my father 'did not even suffer wise men gladly'). Invariably, his way of ending any unpleasant discussion, especially those about life's more undesirable consequences, and even more especially about any consequences that somehow implicated him, was to repeat an increasingly tiresome maxim that surfaces in *Jeffrey Bernard Is Unwell*: 'If you can't take a joke, you shouldn't have joined.' It was therefore with something approaching shock that Sarah and I discovered, on raising the lid of the metal trunk, an unruly, sliding pile of paper and cardboard, which on closer inspection proved to be every greetings card, postcard, Christmas list, letter or childhood piece of doggerel we three children had ever given him, from our first backward-lettered, crayoned efforts on thick, coloured paper to the later letters we sent from abroad as young adults – and the occasional draft of his own. Working through this pile took us many days, as forgotten episodes of our childhoods – holidays, Christmases, Father's Days, misadventures at schools – returned in the vivid retrospective said to come to people when they drown, and by the time we eventually neared the bottom our throats were as dried by emotion as by dusty papers. But on the floor of the trunk was a large white piece of cardboard which lay face down. When we had prised it out we discovered it to be a sign, hand-lettered in thick capitals. It read: 'If you can't take a joke, you shouldn't have joined.'

So, as we'd overlooked the treasures in *How to Live to Be* 22, it was not without a sense of profound irony that I came to find myself, a couple of years later, sitting at a special book rest in a conference room in the British Library, turning the pages with great care and with the aid of a special snake-weight to keep it open, under the supervising eye of Zoë Wilcox, Curator of Modern Literary and Theatrical Manuscripts. My father, who loved libraries, would have been amused – and, more secretly, proud.

Just as 'the tram rattling arteries running through the city centre' of Leeds provided my father, as a boy, with the landmarks by which he orientated an itinerant boyhood, so in *How to Live to Be* 22 there can be discerned various, crisscrossing routes that resurface in *Billy Liar* and in the columns he wrote for the *Daily Mirror* and then the *Daily Mail* for thirty-nine years. His goal in writing the book is to become a proper writer, and not just a cub reporter: when he wonders if his teachers and friends will read the results (even though, as he confesses, their author hasn't: 'I couldn't read my own book now if you paid me to'), he adds: 'will they say, coo, is this all he has to offer, and it isn't.' And it wasn't. But he is not yet aware, as he recalls self-consciously stuffing his pockets with paperbacks and obsessively searching stationers for the right kind of notebook, of the goldmine into which he has begun to tap: he will write, he says, about what he knows, and what he knows best is his own youthful predilection for making things up:

> I dropped the 'Estate' from my address on Halton Moor Estate, so that 'Halton Moor' sounded like heather and fox hounds rather than a housing estate.
> I raised my greengrocer father from the dead, made him captain of a destroyer cruising, somewhat unaccountably, the English Channel, and killed him off again with glory.

Whatever the opposite of a chameleon might be, my father seems, at twenty-two, to have been it, as one point of his elaborate fabrications was not to blend in but to set himself up in direct polar opposition to whomever he hoped to impress – or annoy. Climbing the social ladder one year, for example, he slides down it the next:

> I not only replaced the Estate after Halton Moor but I
> inserted the word 'housing' between Moor and Estate so
> that no one should have any doubt ... that we had only
> recently moved there from the slums.

The episodes surrounding his father, along with a fondness for affecting a limp and conducting an orchestra with a ruler, resurface in Billy Liar:

> 'Well, for instance, there's that bit about my father. Him
> being a sea captain.'
> In a weak moment, or rather in a panoramic series of
> weak moments, I had told the Witch that during the War
> my old man had been the captain of a destroyer ... one
> of the first men to be captured by U-Boats, as a matter
> of fact – and had spent three years in a prisoner of war
> camp. He had been wounded in the leg, which still gave
> him trouble.
> 'You mean he wasn't a sea captain, I suppose?' asked
> the Witch, and I was surprised that *she* didn't seem
> surprised.
> 'He wasn't even in the navy,' I said.

A girl my father calls The Witch, aka Margaret, is also recalled in How to Live, and her rejection of my father's advances ('it seems indecent somehow') as he attempts to seduce her with a Passion Pill concealed in a squashed chocolate recurs almost verbatim in Billy's relationship with Barbara in Billy

Liar, as does another girl's vision of married life in a cottage in Devon, which my father, who would go into withdrawal the moment he lost sight of a smoking factory chimney or the Leeds Bovril sign, appears to have encouraged. Like Billy, and with similarly Machiavellian motives, my father also permitted himself to be called 'lamb.' The cruelty with which these girls are described in turn ('I got me another ugly head') might be balanced by the desperate determination with which my father set about losing his virginity, but if the fibs told to them were designed to seduce, like the rhetoric of Marvell's 'To His Coy Mistress', they lacked a certain appeal: my father told one girl that he owned a budgie that ate oats, and kept up this pointless falsehood 'for months and months and months and months and months.'

My father was born in 1929, in Hunslet, and the poverty in which the family lived during the depression was actually acute. He was the youngest of five children: his father, Ernest, was a hard-drinking costermonger who died when my father was small, leaving the family in the care of the Board of Guardians; his grandparents could neither read nor write; and his brother, Kenneth, became the breadwinner at fourteen (my father, at fourteen, attended the College of Commerce, and not, as he says in *How to Live*, a string factory). His mother did indeed return a stamp to the post office so that she could buy a tin of sardines, and her tenacity in raising her children, and the ways in which she encouraged her youngest by spending her meagre resources on, of all things, second-hand, bound copies of Punch as well as public school stories and other books, was all to be the admiring stuff of Mother's Day.

As a boy, my father played with toy theatres and hand-made newspapers (How to Live recalls the Hearst-like belliger-ence with which, seeking to make his feelings clear to a boy with whom he'd taken umbrage, he produced a single front page with the headline WAR in vast capitals), and his wonder at the world of urban children never left him. It would be the basis for his first novel, There Is a Happy Land, whose traces (albeit in its proper form, as the hymn 'There is a green hill far away') we can also find in How to Live:

> There is a happy land far far away
> Where they have jam and bread three times a day,
> Eggs and bacon they don't see,
> They get no sugar in their tea,
> Miles from the familee, far, far away.

Curiously, however, at least one of the exaggerations to which How to Live confesses became ingrained as my father grew older, and that is his memory of the house in Hunslet. His discovery, when researching City Lights, that the house was not a blackened back-to-back but a double-fronted residence that had once belonged to a doctor, and that the move to the Middleton housing estate was occasioned by the demolition of the house to make way for a road rather than to escape a Hogarthian slum, was like that of a Russian revolutionary who learns, while on his way to pelt Cossacks with bricks, that he is related to Czar Nicholas. Likewise, in his later writings, my father often recalled that when the bailiffs came after his father died penniless they took everything but a mattress and a stool for his mother to sit on (and some ornaments she'd hidden under the coal). I briefly wondered, on reading *How to Live*, whether this was a distorted mental Polaroid, like the back-to-back myth, or even a variant on the budgie that ate oats, but the details are less important than my father's impressions of childhood, or rather the way in which he conjured such impressions with words. Were he alive now, I would question my father closely on only one sentence in *How to Live*: 'I gave my father a barrow,' he writes, 'rather than a lorry.' A *lorry*? What lorry? By the time he'd written *City Lights*, he had had a chance to compare his memories with those of surviving relatives, and he recalls not just his father's cart but the names of the three horses that took turns pulling it. Perhaps it was with the later purchase of a lorry that Ernest, in an attempt to modernize his ambitions to be the Cucumber King of Leeds Market, finally went bust, but again the details are less important than his descriptions of his father, which are among the most beautiful he ever wrote:

> One of the ... memories I have of my father is of being
> scooped out of bed in the middle of the night ...,
> swaddled in a potato sack and jogged through sweating
> cobbled streets to the wholesale market on the back of his
> horse and cart.... Whenever I think of Kirkgate Market

I see in my mind's eye what was indelibly stamped on it by that first confused and dreamlike impression – a shimmering crazy mirror montage of burnished scales, brass weights, marble slabs, naphtha lamps, mountains of pomegranates, horses' breath, billy-cans, iron-clad wheels, squashed blood oranges, and big men with pencils behind their ears shouting the price of carrots. My father's cart piled high with replenished produce, I rode home on top of a sack of Brussels sprouts still nibbling my edge of bread and dripping and feeling, as we passed out into the awakening streets, that I had been in a grotto, the personal guest of a wizard.

But what is most striking about *How to Live* is that it is not just the memories but the daydreams and fantasies of childhood that, rather than falling away as my father grows older, mature with him. Here again is *Billy Liar* in miniature:

Later on I would dream of a little world, an island somewhere, inhabited only by boys and girls. I was the boss of it and we had bogies for buses and lemonade bars and we wore uniforms of grey and I wore a high hat like a bearskin but more complicated and I had a lot of decorations and was held in high esteem.

And later on it was a bigger world, probably the size of Lancashire, inhabited only by young people. I was the boss of it. ... And even now that world exists. And sometimes I creep away to it. ...

And I imagine my dramatic rise to power, becoming virtual dictator, yelling abuse at my enemies but slipping shillings to children on the sly. And the films have a *This Modern Age* newsreel about me: 'Genius – or Madman?'

If *How to Live* does not yet see the full comic potential of this material, it sees its poetry and tragicomedy:

> Taking a look at the Great Big World outside one gets, momentarily, stage-fright. Putting this panic and one's ambitions together, one withdraws entirely into the escapist youth club life and makes it into a private world, where one is free to follow the course of one's inclinations and ambitions with confidence.

What distinguishes Billy Fisher from other dreamers (Walter Mitty, for example), and what makes *Billy Liar* a consummate novel of its time, is the intractability with which it marks the North/South divide between working-class austerity and opportunity. Billy does not get on the train to London not just because he is a dreamer but because the apron-strings of class, region, family, and circumstance are all he dares to know, so he retreats into the 'No 1. Thinking' of Ambrosia:

> The ticket collector looked at me.
> 'You getting on this train?' I shook my head. ...
> I began to whistle 'March of the Movies' and to get in step with it... When I got to the War Memorial I transferred my suitcase to my right hand and at the correct moment I saluted with the left – up, two, three, down, two, three, head erect, shoulders back. ...

Unlike Billy, my father got on the train – or rather, deploying a strategy which in itself might have been borrowed from folklore, he walked. Determined to get to Fleet Street, he hatched a plot with his lifelong friend Ray Hill (a frequent name, like that of John Walsh, in *How to Live*) to traverse the 200-plus miles from Leeds to London by foot, thereby guaranteeing himself twelve inches of daily reporting on the experience in the *Yorkshire Evening Post*. (I refer enduring sceptics to the University of Cardiff, which now has the clips.) That London, when he got there, did not in fact instantly reward the adventure with fortune is covered, along with other pain-ful details, in *Streets Ahead*, but there persists in certain quarters of Leeds the conclusion that my father walked to London and thereby got his start in Fleet Street or, just as tellingly, that he made the whole thing up. In fact, through dogged persistence, he over time received in reply to his own inquiries notes from editors suggesting a chat when he was 'next in London', but unlike Billy, whose letter from the comedian Danny Boon suggests the same idea, my father used further ruses to ensure that he was 'next in London' often, thus securing, with a probationary post on *The Daily Mirror*, enough of a toehold to motivate my mother to pack everything and follow him.

That move was, of course, a seismic shift, and in making it my father joined an entire generation of northern and working-class writers, actors, and directors that included not just Willis Hall but Peter O'Toole, Tom Courtenay, Albert Finney, Arnold Wesker, John Braine, Alan Sillitoe and Stan Barstow. *How to Live* already suggests an awareness of this tectonic rumbling happening in British society when it summarizes the politics of a young man (the thinly disguised author) in 1951 as 'anti-everything,' and recalls a manifesto of sorts to an imagined 'Percy' of highbrow taste, warning him that 'Jones down the road likes Homer. He shifts coal for a living.' The disaffected, post-war generation, usually said to be epitomized by John Osborne's Jimmy Porter, is here in embryo in *How to Live*:

> To hell with it. To hell with the Labour Party, the Liberal Party, the Conservative Party and the Communist Party.
> To hell with Mr. Attlee, Mr. Clement Davies, Mr. Churchill, and Mr. Phil Piratin, who I don't think is their equivalent in Communism but is the only name I can think of at the moment. ...
> I've had a bellyful.

This ability to catch the quicksilver of an era in a single sentence is one of the finest hallmarks of *How to Live*, and the manuscript even exhibits a tell-tale penchant for nostalgia (it ends by evoking my father's lifelong love of trams). Here is *How to Live* on the end of the Phoney War: 'It happened all of a sudden, the way the war suddenly became War.' On the disaffected transition from peace to austerity: 'and the sandbags began to go rotten, and eventually they took them away'. And on the impact of war on the young author:

> I got fed up of gasmasks and rationing and started wondering if the Germans would ever land here, and I wanted to be able to buy a lot of Holland toffee again, and I wanted to see my brothers again, and the lights in town, and everything.

And here is my father forty-three years later in *City Lights*:

> ... deprived of a proper Blitz and nights spent in a deep
> shelter singing 'Run, Rabbit, Run', my interest in the war
> began to pall. Austerity and the blackout became a bore.
> I began to pine for the city lights, for the flag-bedecked
> illuminated trams which had plied Briggate and City Square.

It will be several years before my father actually meets the *Mirror's* Cassandra in a pub and rather tactlessly informs him that he intends to inherit his column, but in *How to Live* there are traces of the voice that will make his own columns a selling point on the front page ('Keith Waterhouse – page 8'). Although *How to Live* recalls alarming political swings and Damascene conversions to Conservatism, socialism, anti-unionism, and 'an almost homosexual love of the miners,' what is most striking is the force of such convictions and the authority and wit of the young, first-person singular. Here is a debate in *How to Live* about politics with a fellow conscript in the air force in a passage that anticipates the mature columns' commonsensical satires of 'The Department of Guesswork,' my father's name for any policy or position, usually government-sponsored, backed by statistics:

> Early on in the arguments I created a catalogue of entirely
> fictitious statistics and quotations, ranging from the
> number of unemployed men who died from starvation
> during the General Strike to what Mr. Churchill had said
> about the dockers on numerous occasions. Most of these
> went out of my head as soon as they were quoted, but as

my opponent's memory was as short as mine I was able to put the figure of leading British conservatives who had supported the war at twenty on one day and five hundred the next, without anyone noticing any difference.

The strategy is especially useful when the twenty-two-year-old finds himself battling the provincial racism, anti-Semitism, and 'anti-homosexualism' rife in post-war Leeds, and the passages in which he recalls standing up for 'the minorities' (as though 'the minorities' – 'the black, the Jew, and the sodomite' – were a trio of whimpering boys being bullied at school), date *How to Live to Be* 22 even more surely than the accounts of milk bars or austerity. Although he realizes that the stand he took on such occasions was hardly cosmopolitan ('Negroes are just as intelligent as we are because look at Paul Robeson'), it's a stark reminder of the world he inhabited:

> I produced figures, even where none existed, against people who claimed there were no Jewish roadmenders, that the Jews never joined the Army, that they never went down the mines, that Jewish businessmen controlled half the factories in Leeds. Ho no they don't, I said....

In 'ho no they don't,' I can hear my father's voice especially clearly, and, more significantly, I can hear him having a lot of fun. 'This is nobody's style but my own,' he writes, though in fact one sometimes hears his style emerging from a number of other influences: there are, at various points, shades of Hemingway, Crompton's *William* books, Dylan Thomas, W.W.

Jacobs, James Thurber, George Orwell, Evelyn Waugh, Arnold Bennett, and, above all, Edgar Wallace and P.G. Wodehouse. Wallace (whose adventures my father absorbed through Margaret Lane's biography, to which he frequently returned throughout his life) was to become his hero, and the statue commemorating him in Fleet Street ('...but to Fleet Street he gave his heart') became for my father as giant a landmark for the would-be-journalist headed to the South as the Angel of the North is to northbound travellers today. Wodehouse, just as crucially, made him laugh. It appears at first to be a paradoxical influence, as the public schools of Mike, Psmith and his chums and the London clubs of the Eggs, Beans, and Crumpets could not have been further from Osmondthorpe Council School and Leeds youth clubs, but my father admired Wodehouse's ability to craft imaginary worlds and hilarious single sentences (which he could quote word for word), and above all his astounding output, which represented a professional writer making books with the skilled tireless-ness of a tradesman. (When my father and Willis Hall went into partnership, the prolific ease with which they seemed to produce scripts earned their office the nickname of the Word Factory, and they toyed with the idea of renting a van with the words 'Scripts Written While you Wait' on the side. My father's lifetime insistence, in his later, solo years, on hammering each day at a typewriter long after computers had rendered typewriters obsolete, always struck me as his masochistic identification of writing with manual labour.)

The public school story, much imitated, was an entire genre in itself, and when, in *How to Live*, my father admits to experimenting with his by-line and his final decision to drop his middle initial, he already, if unwittingly, has the raw material for the stalled story Billy Fisher tinkers with while working as an undertaker's clerk:

'I say, weed! Aren't you a new bug?' Sammy Brown turned to greet the tall, freckle faced boy who walked across the quad towards him. Sammy's second name was appropriate – for the face of this sturdy young fellow was as brown as a berry. W. Fisher. William Fisher. The Two Schools at Gripminster, by William Fisher. William L. Fisher. W.L. Fisher. Two-School Sammy, by W.L.P. Fisher. Two Schools at Gripminster: A Sammy Brown Story by W.L.P. Fisher. The Sammy Brown Omnibus. W. Lashwood Fisher. W. de L. Fisher.

How to Live to Be 22 also tells of the influence of the classics, or rather it confesses to my father's predilection for rating classics he had not read in an artistic venture he called The Queer Book – named, in a rare lapse of worldliness, in imitation of the Yellow Book, which he had never read either. 'Most of them I didn't even possess,' he writes, adding that the list offered opinions on

'Something – anything – by Eden Phillpotts' (I had never read anything – something – by Eden Phillpotts...)
    'Something of Conrad's – say *Rescue*' (Say *Rescue* if you will, but I have not read it.)

He also mastered knowing what 'was on the Third Pro-gramme without once listening to it.'

The ability to absorb such things without necessarily read-ing or listening to them was to serve him all his life, and not just in the jubilant conviction with which, after several glasses of wine, his voice mounting in joyous triumph while his hands hovered above his head like a pair of manic hummingbirds, my father continued to enjoy arguments about subjects on which he was no authority whatsoever. Post Google, it is hard to appreciate how unreadily even an affected acquaintance with horizons beyond one's own might be had by someone on an austerity-era northern housing estate, but as a boy my father, so he writes in City Lights, was 'a weird child,' as addicted to exploring Leeds with a view to 'seeing what was around the next corner' as to telling his mother tall tales about where he'd been. (Not a far cry from dreaming about what lay beyond.) I sometimes think that on these boyhood explorations he must have crossed paths with some urban, soot-caked sprite, who gave him the lifelong ability to absorb, through a kind of metropolitan osmosis, all the detailed minutiae of life's passing show, its sounds and sights and smells, and then to re-conjure them with words. It was no wonder that his mother 'was a little frightened' of him or that what distinguished his lifetime working friendship with Willis Hall was the ability to communicate through 'telepathy.' In City Lights my father recalls, how, when he was a boy, his mother claimed she was taking him to see

Mickey Mouse: she took him, in fact, to St. James' Hospital to be circumcised, and while recuperating in the ward with other boys, 'snugly cocooned in what no one had yet learned to call the inner city,' he soaked up his impressions like a sponge:

> All day I could hear the clanging of trams and at night the shunting of trains from the nearby marshalling yards, and in the small hours the parish church clock chiming, and in the morning the clatter of horse's hooves, the rumble of wagons and lorries, the distant street cries from the Market, the droning trams again, the factory hooters, the clanking of brewers' drays delivering their crates and barrels, the small thunder of cattle on their way to the slaughterhouse, the revving up of buses, the shouts of the newsvendors, the voices of workmates exchanging banter, the bolting back of doors, the whistling of porters and errand boys, the rat-a-tat of postmen, the far-off tinkling of the arcade carillons, and all the instruments of the city, brass, timpani and woodwind that gradually orchestrated themselves into the concerto of the day-long hubbub.

The miraculous ease with which everything – changing fads and fashions, idioms, mores, colloquialisms (former Punch editor Alan Coren likened his gift for dialogue to a mynah bird's) and, most especially, the contents of every newspaper and news programme, which he devoured daily – seemed to seep through his pores and onto the page became especially valuable in later life. One day, when in his seventies, and following an especially long lunch

21

with fellow journalists, my father fell and broke his right shoulder, and was briefly confined, for the first time since the Mickey Mouse episode, to hospital. From there, unable to use his right hand, he dictated his next column to Stella Bingham. Stella reported that what came out of his mouth was exactly 840 words, or column length. Once discharged, he was soon back at work, but his confidence in walking the streets – 'mooching' as my father called these perambulations, an aimless wandering through 'the passing show' of London that allowed him turn over plot lines and characters' speeches in his head, often with an animation that startled passers-by – gradually diminished. As he neared eighty, his ability to navigate the uneven paving stones and treacherous tree roots of 'the Royal Borough of Earl's Court' diminished also, and despite a brief, hazardous phase of going out to dinner or the pub in his slippers (at least one establishment took exception to his wild-haired, unkempt appearance), his preferred station at the end of his sofa, an open bottle of wine at his side and a yellow legal pad and an uncapped pen in front of him, became so much a part of his *modus operandi* that he found various excuses to stop going out altogether.

Then the gift of osmosis came into its own. Though the twice-weekly *Daily Mail* columns of his last years (he retired at eighty, and died a few months later) still managed to convey the impression that he was present, with the promptness of the reporter and the sagacity of the essayist, in tube stations, pubs and supermarkets, catching the voices, sounds, sights, and smells on the coat sleeves of time and place as they bustled by, they were written while he sat on the sofa in his second-floor flat, his gaze turned towards the window, stirring only to sip at a glass of wine or brush a wisp of wild, white hair from his temple as, in minute detail, he absorbed through the sounds of the wet traffic below the scandal or folly of the day and turned it, in his head, into 840 words.

But by the end of *How to Live to Be* 22 everything – London, *There Is a Happy Land*, *Billy Liar*, Willis Hall, *A Kind of Loving*, Hitchcock and *Torn Curtain*, Peter O'Toole, Albert Finney, Tom Courtenay, Julie Christie, David Frost, Ned Sherrin – is little more than a decade away. For the time being, he is twenty-two, and it is no wonder that when he looks out of the window his 'insides turn to liquid with an absurd and frothy delight.' He will have, as he predicts, 'always one book or play on the go like people who always have the kettle on the gas,' and the neon lights that lit his name up in the clouds will be 'bigger and brighter than before'.

HOW TO LIVE TO BE 22

INTRODUCTION

I was once told by someone who probably lifted it from a book that one cannot write about the sea unless one has been to sea, that one cannot write about life in prison unless one has been to prison.

Without thinking a great deal about the accuracy of that maxim I wondered what I personally had done which, having done it, I could write about.

I discovered that I had done nothing at all except live for twenty-two consecutive years.

The decision to write a book on the experience of reaching the age of twenty-two came, of course, not as a logical development of what I had been told about writing but as a blinding brainwave, so brilliant that it fascinated me.

Ideas like that come very frequently at this age. They are always perfect, always priceless, and they are half the fun of being twenty-two. In young authors they almost always result in a cupboardful of first chapters.

But this idea was different. The brainwave comet burnt itself out, but the idea stayed.

I knew eventually that this idea was going to take me past the first-chapter stage in book writing.

I could tell that because I knew that for the first time in my life I had a story of my own to tell. I also knew that I could tell the truth.

When you are twenty-two it is usually very difficult to tell the truth – which is why those first chapters in the cupboard are so full of insincerities.

But it is even more difficult to keep on telling lies – which is why so many first chapters are discarded anyway.

This book can only be finished because I can tell the truth the whole way through.

I am ready to admit that I have not written this book as the story of mankind at twenty-two or to spread the Message of Youth, whatever that is, through the world.

I have written it for the same reason that any young man of twenty-two writes a book: because I am in a sustained coma of industrious exuberance at having got a good idea, because my friends are going to wish that they had thought of it first, and because people are going to pay me a great many compliments about it.

That is not being conceited – it is being twenty-two years old.

Of course, someone will probably see this as the story of mankind at twenty-two, and they will probably find the Message of Youth in what I have written.

I shall be very pleased if they do, for then I shall think I am very deep indeed.

PART ONE

I used to own a snapshot that was considered so good in the youth club it concerned that the chemist who did the developing made more money doing enlargements of it than out of a whole church wedding of photogenics.

The subject of the snapshot was the club's hiking group on its arrival, with many a joke about buses and who had eaten whose sandwiches, at journey's end.

The group was arranged, for the sake of symmetry, around a pile of crags consisting of one small rock perched on top of a larger one, like the tiers of a wedding cake.

Half a dozen people, standing boy next to girl, boy next to girl, were sized off around the base rock, leaning back on it as though they were riding surfboards. Another four stood on top of it, leaning back against the upstairs rock. The business was rounded off by a single person who was placed on top of the upper rock like a flag on a sandcastle.

Seen through the viewfinder, the completed effect was of a pyramid of somewhat self-conscious human beings.

The most self-conscious of the lot was the one on top, the one I am coming to.

He was big, broad, bronzed, fit, alert. All six feet of him stood erect and rigid, jaw set with all the determination of adolescence. His head high, he was staring with peculiar intensity and fervour at some object off the picture, probably mythical.

Small wonder that we christened this picture 'The Pyramid of Youth' and wondered why the low-circulation week-lies devoted to art, politics, the future and other obscure fountains of inspiration did not reproduce it as their front cover.

The reason they never did, as I have since discovered, is that they already have it. Or something like it. The horn-rimmed weeklies have so many pictures like 'The Pyramid of Youth' that they could fill every page, never mind the cover, with pyramids of youth until their asthmatic circulations finally petered out.

Not all these pictures follow the same pattern, though they observe the same general rule. Some of them are of a ruddy, clean-living lad standing legs apart upon a field of wheat stubble, holding a muck rake at an artistic angle and staring keenly at a point three feet above the photographer's head, or three feet above where the photographer's head would have been if he hadn't been lying on his belly in order to

29

get the boy big and prominent on a general background of rural enterprise.

Some of them are of a girl at the seaside: not the usual flirt and candy floss seaside, but the bleak part where poets and murderers abound in books. And she too is gawping in the customary thoughtful fashion. And so is the young man standing with his back to us, hands clenched, on what is apparently the brink of the earth at sunrise. And so are the boy and girl together on top of a hill with a small and scruffy and smoky town beneath them. And so is the top bit of our 'Pyramid of Youth'.

They are as familiar to my eye as the Whistling Boy. More familiar. I do not know what the Whistling Boy is supposed to represent. But I know what they are supposed to represent – Youth, Youth, the spirit of Youth. With a capital Y.

Youth, the trustees of posterity (Disraeli).

Youth, like summer morn (Shakespeare).

Youth, life's beautiful moment (Lacordaire).

Youth, to whom was given so much of earth, so much of heaven (Wordsworth).

Youth, whose hope is high, who dost to truth inspire (Robert Bridges).

Youth! Youth!

I have never heard anything so damn silly in all my life.

What do you think the top bit of our pyramid is? An organiser, a leader of men? A boy with the future in front of him? A boy with hopes and high ambitions and poetry in his soul? A boy of faith and depth and integrity, today's apprentice and the master of tomorrow?

Youth! Youth!

Actually his immediate ambition is to own a motorbike. His main concern is to get rid of the spots on his face, and to learn a passable foxtrot. Professionally he is a cleaner of windows and his professional aspiration is to clean fewer windows for more money; politically he is anti-everything; poetically he is inclined towards the Red Circle School stories in *The Wizard*. His last reflection on his Maker was a muttered 'Christ' as he missed a rung on the ladder one day – not the ladder to eternal fame, but the ladder to a first floor window where he might with luck see a girl in her underclothes.

Youth! Youth! Hail, blooming Youth!

I would not have begun like that if I hadn't just been reading a book by Noel Coward. I am not really bitter or superior about the Youth myth, really I don't give a damn, just putting it on.

I should have begun with a cool-headed examination of the way in which that word Youth is used, and why it is used, and who uses it.

Something like this way:–

It is used as a middle-twentieth-century substitute for the Union Jack, England dear England and his Gracious Majesty the King. It came in when we got sick of Kipling and music hall patriotism.

It is used because however much we cringe at Tommy

31

Atkins and the never-setting sun we cannot do without them for very long. We are a race of peacocks, and we are bigger peacocks for believing that we are not. (Don't we love to hear foreigners talk about 'the mad English', for instance, and when they don't talk about us – which they don't, as a matter of fact, most of the time – don't we love to point out to each other what the foreigners have said already?) So after we had spewed up the *Barrack-room Ballads* we looked round for something else to pin our pageantry on. This was the age of young people, so it became the Age of Youth.

It is used, this word Youth, by statesmen, ministers of religion, editors of newspapers, writers of pageants, narrators in the more pompous broadcast feature programmes and sound tracks of documentaries about the present age. It is used a great deal by young people themselves who got it in the first place from L. du Garde Peach.

Some of the people who use this word know perfectly well that they are talking through their hats; others are quite sincere about it. Some use it because they have only had dealings with the word through reading it in the context that other people have given it, and imagine it to mean what they have been told it means – hope and glory.

They are all, whatever their reasons, wrong...

Yes, that is how I should have begun.

Then I would have reached the same conclusion that I have reached anyhow, which is that Youth as a word is very debased indeed.

God and the King, Empire Sunday and forty-seven legions of organised and representative young people lined up to form the word Progress (or even Youth) on a background of park-green – they come into Youth all right. But they come in with about five hundred other things and they are only a part of the picture, a part which tarnishes rather more quickly than some of the others.

Youth, the real youth, is a mosaic, and it is made up of many things, some of them fairly disgusting.

It is made of conceit, which dresses youth up in a silk tie and is the sole reason that he climbs up on a rock and looks like Youth.

It is made of sex, newly discovered, which puts a rather nasty angle on the fresh, clean-cut maiden in the sweeping skirt halfway down the Pyramid of Youth.

It is made of sex the accomplished fact, which puts night school (including the Future) down the drain.

It is made of sex the improbable future, which accounts for about forty per cent of youth's young daydream.

It is made of daydreaming, the other sixty per cent: wild ideas which might be anything from winning the Battle of Britain single-handed to becoming Prime Minister – all following exactly the same pattern as the bubble-pipe dreams of Richmal Crompton's William.

It is made of selfishness, which youth covers up in a variety of more attractive cloaks, from worldly wisdom to cynicism, so that if he does not want to waste twopence on the Waifs and Strays he can say roundly that flag days are a menace to Socialism, or anything else he pleases.

It is made of self-love, which is why youth can pass half a dozen blind beggars by, then glow with satisfaction for a fortnight after giving a shilling to the seventh.

It is made of humbug, which is why youth can believe implicitly at any given moment that he is a Fascist or a Communist or an atheist or a Catholic or in love or not in love – or even that Youth is humbug, or that it is not humbug at all.

It is made of laziness, which is why youth will very often not take a bath or help his mother.

It is made of action, which is the job youth does in his more serious moments, when he is youth no longer, when he is tucked away in a quiet corner translating some of his ambitions from heaven to earth, when – if he happens to be that sort of person – he is carving a future for himself, not with flags and bugles but with his bare hands, just (oddly enough) like the pictures of Youth at work.

Of all these things, sugar and spice and puppy dogs' tails, youth is made.

I was born in 1929, and I came to be twenty-two in 1951.

It makes people of twenty-two feel good and old to know that the world of 1929 and onwards was a vastly different place to the world of 1951.

Arthur Askey was sweeping the country, as they say, with *Band Waggon*. Not in 1929, but in the first days I remember of that golden age. We hadn't a wireless in those days, we couldn't afford one, so I never heard *Band Waggon*, but I was in the habit of picking up bits of information from other boys and passing them back as though I had them first hand, so that I could tell a boy, '*Band Waggon*'s finishing next week' two days after he had told me, and he would say, 'I know!' scornfully, but I didn't mind the sneer because he did think we had a wireless.

And things weren't scarce like they are now, because I can remember buying Holland toffee with fourpence that I stole from my mother, and it lasted an enormously long time, long enough for me to get fed up of it, and a girl called Pearl Hetherington took me shopping for her mother, and she bought some fig biscuits and gave me one.

And Christmas was more Christmassy, because the pillar boxes were so full of cards that they got choked up and the envelopes came spilling out of the slot, and there were Santa Clauses made of soap and chocolate, and carols, and the shops seemed to be open till midnight.

And there was a war in China and a civil war in Spain, and the civil war was the most exciting because I imagined men in serge suits shooting each other.

And there were more Scouts and Cubs and Guides about, because I was one of them, and there was more of the *Chums Annual*, tea and muffins atmosphere about – nobody reads school stories nowadays.

And people were religious, because I was in the choir

at the Holy Cross church, which we used to call the 'Holy Hoss'. I got in by singing 'There is a green hill far away' and I wore a purple surplice (or is it a hassock?) while the others wore black, and I was very surprised when they paid me ninepence at the end of the month.

And they had small coaches the shape of a D with the flat side uppermost, black ones driven by black horses, for funerals.

And we all ran to the top of the street to see our first double-decker bus.

And things were cheaper, because I got a shilling for golf caddying and I was able to take my mother to a music hall with it to see someone who was very famous.

And everyone was poor, because a newspaper was running a Boots for the Bairns fund, and I was sent to the Silverdale Poor Children's Holiday Camp, and I hated it and looked wistfully across the bay at, I believe, Morecambe, where we would have gone if we hadn't been charity.

And there was going to be a war, and I hoped there would be, and there was.

And the women looked ridiculous in the clothes they wore, because I have seen some magazines that were published in the Thirties and that is what they looked like.

And, of course, over there where you see houses was all fields when I was a lad...

When Chamberlain said he was going to start the war – we had got a wireless by then – I was sitting on the garden gate of the house we had just moved to on a new housing estate. I was more thrilled about living in a house after a downstairs flat than about the war.

War meant that school was closed for the longest holiday I have ever had – so long that it got boring, like the Holland toffee. It meant the blackout, and A.R.P., and catchy songs, and gasmasks, and air raid sirens, and my brothers getting called up, and me trying on their tin hats and hitting myself over the head with the poker because it didn't hurt with a tin hat on, and ration books, and notices about careless talk

And the L.D.V., which I can't remember standing for anything else except 'Look, duck and vanish'. And the most unlikely people joined the L.D.V. And we knew a barber who had rushed away in the middle of shaving a customer to join it, just like you read about in the newspapers, and just as, in fact, we did read about when the newspapers got to know about him.

It was a sentimental, music-hall war, what with Vera Lynn and Garrison Theatre and evacuees and waste paper and hanging our washing on the Siegfried Line – and the L.D.V.

It happened all of a sudden, the way the war suddenly became War.

I got fed up of gasmasks and rationing and started wondering if the Germans would ever land here, and I wanted to be able to buy a lot of Holland toffee again, and I wanted to see my brothers again, and the lights in town, and everything.

The L.D.V. changed its name to the Home Guard. And the music-hall war suddenly petered out and became a serious theatre war, and I found myself growing up.

And all the children of the war were growing up around me, changing as completely as the L.D.V. when they made it the Home Guard and put away the pikes.

In order to be twenty-two you must first have been seventeen.

Getting to be twenty-two happens like this: first, you are seventeen. Seventeen brings with it a number of gaudy impressions and ideas that are so sickly that by the time you are nineteen you have had a bellyfull.

So at nineteen you become a reactionary to everything you thought at seventeen. Everything you think is dynamically and deliberately opposed to everything you thought at seventeen – but you think it in just the same gaudy way.

By the time you are twenty-one you have had another kind of reaction. You are sick to death of everything you have thought ever since you began to think at all. You numb your brain with inertia, but being young you cannot keep things out of your head.

Gradually your mind fills up with a number of ideas, some of them familiar to you, some of them old ideas modified, some of them quite new. Then you are twenty-two. What happens after that I do not know. Does one spend one's life getting sick of ideas and bringing in new ones?

But first you have got to be seventeen.

38

The war went from L.D.V. to Home Guard, and the sand-bags began to go rotten, and eventually they took them away, and the Home Guard was disbanded, and the war was over, and I was seventeen.

Being seventeen meant for me the discovery of the fol-lowing gaudy canvasses in my attic of a brain:—

Politics,

Art,

Coffee,

The English Grammar.

Each of these pictures, which I lugged out long before the cobwebs had time to settle, was a mosaic with a different idea in every piece (just like Youth).

Except the politics one, which was surprisingly simple.

At sixteen I had already discovered my King and Country, and had gone through an intense period of nauseating patriot-ism, going to the length of standing up in the house when they played 'God Save the King' on the wireless, and on V.E. day telling two drunken Canadians who were shouting 'Canada for ever' not to forget Good Old Britain, to which they answered 'Balls'.

At seventeen, however, I discovered Cynicism (this comes under Coffee in the picture of ideas, and I will deal with it as a whole later). Cynicism was fascinating, new born; I had to do something with it.

I wired Cynicism and Patriotism together and produced the Conservative Party.

I joined the Young Conservatives, attending four or five times and never paying any subscription. (At seventeen one is inordinately proud of not paying any subscriptions, boasting of not having paid them long after one has, on the sly, forked out. This also comes under Coffee.)

It was wonderful to saunter into the Conservative Club, being condescending to the porter and wondering if he thought I was rich. I got the same feeling as I had as a child when I would put on a limp to make people think I had a wooden leg.

Out of the haze of Conservatism I can remember the Corn Laws and the word 'doctrinaire'. But it is Flannel Dance which I remember most.

Flannel Dance was my key to the other side of the tracks. It was the main battle in a fairly sordid personal war against being poor, or rather against living on a housing estate, which seemed far more disgraceful.

This private war had been going on in a lazy sort of way for some time. I had been jogging along pronouncing aitches, saying 'Yes' in that silly way that Yorkshiremen so used to saying 'Yur' adopt when they are swanking, and I had just got to that point of craftiness where, instead of persuading my mother to let me wear my brother's best suit to go to the Conservatives in, I would cheerfully wear an old sports coat disguised by a don't-give-a-damn-for-conventional-dress scowl. Then along came Flannel Dance.

How it happened was that the secretary of the entertainment

committee asked me if I would like a ticket for this Flannel Dance.

That was what did it. I had not the faintest idea what a Flannel Dance was, but I knew that it was something superior to a dinner dance, and I knew that the sports-coat-and-scowl routine had paid a dividend.

I was enormously proud. No-one had ever asked me to buy a ticket to a dinner dance under the impression that I possessed evening dress. But this man was inviting me to a Flannel Dance under the impression not only that I had the right apparel for a Flannel Dance, but that I actually knew what a Flannel Dance was and was quite used to this sort of thing.

My cup was full. No-one who has not been seventeen and out of the bottom drawer can imagine how far more delightful it is to be invited to an informal 'do' than to a formal one. The secretary was saying: 'Here is a dance which is different from what we are all used to because we are leaving the monkey suits in the wardrobe this time. Wear what you've got on.' He was asking me to be informal. And by specially asking me to be informal, he automatically assumed that I spent most of my time being formal. Does that make sense?

I said yes, of course, and dug into my pocket far more eagerly than I need have done. I never went to the Flannel Dance, I daren't, but from this day forward I was a changed man.

He thought I knew how to be formal. He thought I had evening dress. He thought I went to cricket dances and tennis clubs.

All right then. Pronouncing aitches was no longer good enough. I had to have a good address and good family and good clothes and a good school.

I dropped the 'Estate' from my address on Halton Moor Estate, so that 'Halton Moor' sounded like heather and fox hounds rather than a housing estate.

I raised my greengrocer father from the dead, made him captain of a destroyer cruising, somewhat unaccountably, the English Channel, and killed him off again with glory.

I split my two suits and sports coat and flannels up into three pairs of trousers and three coats, so that I had nine different combinations of clothing which I wore on successive days.

Instead of being terrifically proud of having won a scholarship to the Leeds College of Commerce I became mildly apologetic and spoke airily about taking a business course, dropping mention of scholarships altogether.

I began to read Punch.

I have an idea that a great many things go back to Flannel Dance. I ought to be ashamed of having been ashamed of my background. Unfortunately I am not. I think it was a definite climb up the ladder.

The more immediate rungs of that ladder were the perils of Conservative policy. So far, as far as the party line was concerned, I had kept my trap shut.

42

Now, since Flannel Dance, I began to talk. I knew that sneering formed a big part of the Conservative repertoire, so I sneered.

I sneered at The Miners (and it is surprising how much hate one can pack into that gratuitous 'the').

I sneered at the old age pensioners, getting that wonderful pompous self-satisfied squiggly-indignant feeling when I heard some competent Tory say how if one class wants old age pensions, it must not expect to get them out of another class.

I hated people outside the clerical classes, being of the belief that Black Coated Workers Work as Hard as Anyone Else.

On the other hand I loved Mr. Churchill and Mr. Anthony Eden as brothers. I was sorry for highly-taxed rich people, who felt being poor far more than poor people who were used to it felt.

I proved conclusively the menace of Socialism by comparing something that Mr. Strachey had said in one year with something he had said some time else.

Of course, with such slim material to work on my mind got sick pretty soon.

I am glad, though, that I turned to Conservatism and not to Socialism at seventeen. Those whose discovery of politics fetches up on the left side drift into being eighteen by selling pamphlets outside political meetings. I feel that they have missed seventeen, and that they will never live to be twenty-two but only to be a very mature forty.

I turned to Art, involving Oscar Wilde.

I once read an advertisement in *Reveille for the Weekend* which held, quite rightly, that the average man has not time to read the works of Homer, Shakespeare, Milton and several other 'Must' authors in their entirety and enjoy life as well. It advised him to buy this book, a kind of synopsis of the classics, which would give him a working knowledge of them without the tedious business of reading them.

My attitude to Art was like that. I never read anything by Oscar Wilde, but I read Hesketh Pearson's biography of him.

Oh, and I always read his epigrams when they reprinted them as space fillers in the magazine digests, and I even wrote my own:—

'A wife is a platitude, a mistress an epigram.'

I bought *John O'London's*, *The Times Literary Supplement* and the *Observer*, reading the book ads and even some of the brighter articles.

I got acquainted with the *Yellow Book* and Aubrey Beardsley's drawings without having seen either.

I learnt how to pronounce 'aesthetic' and used the word more than once.

I got to know what was on the Third Programme without once listening to it.

I learnt about Clerihews and wrote my own, which I importantly entitled Intellectual Clerihews:—

Oscar Wilde
Got considerably riled
When Meredith, clowning,
Said 'Wilde is a prose Browning – so is Browning.'

And more down to earth ones, to show that I had that necessary connection with the earth without being of the earth:–

Ripley
When tipley
Wouldn't know what
To believe and what not.

I regularly took books of poetry out of the library, but unfortunately never opened them.

I swore that I understood Ezra Pound.

I learnt odd facts about authors so that it sounded as though I knew all about them, such as that George Borrow first saw the light and that Carlyle lost manuscripts, and that someone else worked in a house until it was full of paper and then moved on somewhere else.

I thought Shakespeare thoroughly old-fashioned.

I yearned for a black cloak and a beard.

And in my off moments I collected sixty books by P.G. Wodehouse:

(Jeeves
leaves

young masters who are so ill bred
as to wear lounge suit and a quill tie in bed).

Having read that Samuel Butler said everyone should keep a commonplace book (later wondering which Samuel Butler did say it, being enormously proud of the fact that I knew there were two Samuel Butlers, and later still not giving a damn – and being enormously proud of not giving a damn – how many Samuel Butlers there were), I started to keep one myself.

I called it the Queer Book, which I still think is a good title, but not as good as I thought it was when I was seventeen.

One of the features of the Queer Book was a list of My Fifty Best Books. Most of them I did not even possess.

It included *The Pickwick Papers* by Charles Dickens, which I had never read, and anyway by the time I was nineteen I loathed Dickens, of course.

The Rubaiyat of Omar Khayyam (I bought it, but I have never read it except the bit about the moving finger).

Oscar Wilde's *Dorian Gray* (I called it *Dorian Gray* because I could not remember whether it was *The Portrait of Dorian Gray* or *The Picture of Dorian Gray*. I have never read it).

Shakespeare's *Sonnets* (I have never read any of them).

'Something – anything – by Eden Phillpotts' (I have never read anything – something – by Eden Phillpotts, though I have heard his plays on the wireless, and I do not even know if I have spelt his name right).

Pepys' *Diaries* (I have never read them).

'The whole of the immortal *Forsyte Saga*', which I have never read a word of.

'Something of Conrad's – say *Rescue*.' (Say *Rescue* if you will, but I have not read it.)

No. 50 was as follows: 'And finally – what shall it be? Oliver Wendell Holmes at the breakfast table? Or Owen Seaman? Or the wrath of Achilles in the two dozen books of the epic *Iliad*? I think not, though I'd like to give the place to these and many more...' (I have never read any of them. I cannot now remember who Owen Seaman is.)

I was being deliberately honest with some of the other books when I said I liked music-hall memoirs, P.G. Wodehouse, *Goodbye, Mr. Chips*, James Thurber, the *Just William* books, 1066 *and All That* and a school story by Gunby Hadath. But my honesty was that reactionary kind of honesty – the bluff, blustering honesty of the don who admits that he goes to the pictures to see Betty Grable's legs. No, I was not very honest after all, just conceited, and so was the don.

It got worse. I began to take to university quarterlies. The hate for most people that had come out in my adventures with politics bubbled up again, and this time I believe I called them 'The Throng'. I affected a literary stoop, complete with frown. I perfected a nice trick of holding a book by the centre quire of its pages, so that the two covers and fifty pages on either side hung down in a conspicuously scruffy manner. I never had fewer than four books bulging out of

47

my side pockets, the outside one always having an impressive title visible to the public.

I wrote an obscure short story called *The Statue*, written after I had dreamt of climbing up a monument after Bernard Shaw (who at seventeen I called a shocking writer):–

'Although the man was an artist, he had no art. He could not write, he could not paint. He knew nothing of music, he could appreciate nothing. The man as he thought about literature thought of Swinburne and Balzac and Brieux, but they were only names. And as he thought of the drama he thought of miniature theatres and 'The Bells', which meant nothing. What he had heard in Bloomsbury he knew; but the kind of thing heard in Bloomsbury is Dutch to all but those who know it already. And so when the man thought about art he thought of Whistler and Wilde's epigrams on the Academy, and when he thought of music he thought of some hostess's sweeping observations on Sibelius. But what the man knew was nothing, and the man was nobody...'

That was me, that was. The story went on to tell how the man had the urge to climb up a statue ('Climbing a statue? No! Living! Being! Conquering!') which he did, only it unfortunately snapped just as he reached the top.

I could not get much further than this in Art, but there was one more mile to go. When I was nearly eighteen I gathered all my obscure artistic forces around me and perpetrated the following poem:–

48

Eighteen

Wafted still unwonted free
of cunning deft to warp against the rush
so green beneath the darkened blue
a parched but burning green in second flush
and reaching as a twice-ringed tree,

however, new in measure; floating so
a new dimension of uncornered shape
evolved and stands unrooted yet
and so untethered stays until the crow
of morning brings the night black drape.

Ended high in laurel'd ease
but viewing tense all knowing of the gone
and skilled, for set and known by he
who strengthened stills himself or shall buoy on
who moves and looked on also sees

the bearing stands judicial choosing none
a scale by which the lesser take the grade
and shift aside or choose for fame
the flotsam of the land where of anon
a rock of living space is made.

Winded in the blown green
is moving watched though withered in the mist.
The blast will stop in span and sharp,
the world will gather up another gist
and weigh not what the weighed have seen

But casting rash sling out the burning low
and choose the lambent flamed but whitened arc.
Thus quick but true the settled rise.
The left bereft and damped of lesser glow
fall back unbounded in the dark.

Phew. Then I sank back exhausted. That was that. There was nothing more to do. There were occasional lapses, such as wanting to write a book entirely in italics, but it was never the same again. Gradually, art went the way of politics and of all flesh.

All this time Coffee had been going on.

Coffee is to the English teenager what Coca Cola is to the American, but it is more significant.

Until he is seventeen the average youth does not touch coffee at all, at least not in lower-class circles. There is something very bourgeois about coffee, just as there is about eating bread that has been cut from corner to corner instead of straight across.

But by seventeen the average youth has joined the average youth club, and he drinks enough coffee to have a bath in.

It is a little difficult to explain, but it is definitely all to do with being seventeen.

First, people have got by nature to sit at tables and drink things when they are of the age, temperament or station to have time on their hands. Seventeen is well past the lemonade stage, and so the drink is coffee.

Second, there is this bourgeois business. Every seventeen-year-old is at heart a snob, seeing himself as a playboy or an intellectual idler. Drinking coffee fits in with that.

Third, there is something grown up about coffee, so it quickly becomes an obsession. But because at seventeen one has to stand on the roof and shout to the world what one is doing, one has to get up and shout that one is drinking coffee. This can be done by getting a name for drinking about a quart of coffee a day, or by getting a name for never paying for the coffee, or by insisting on stopping at every cafe during a club hike. Similarly with cigarettes – smoking being a very grown up habit, one has to draw attention to it by pretending to be desperate for a cigarette, by smoking only Markovitch, by constantly cadging cigarettes and, at one stage or another, smoking a pipe.

And so in seventeen-year-old society coffee is mentioned many times a day, usually with a capital C: 'Come for a Coffee, how many Coffees have you had, let's have another Coffee (we've had three already, aren't we pigs?').

I drank my coffee, cadged my cigarettes and smoked my pipe along with the rest of them, and followed the same pursuits that are bound up so closely with coffee:–

Cynicism. Being cynical was a delightful experience. It involved being rude to everyone and making long lists of 'People I dislike':–

Tenants who boast of having been in their house twenty-five years without owing a week's rent; tram conductors who have read of the humour of cockney bus conductors and try to imitate them; men who, no matter how full the bus that has just passed, insist that there was room for at least half a dozen; those who argue most about politics – the people who know least what they are talking about; women who force conversation ('If they must talk, let them read and be intelligent and notice things, then they can talk about interesting things'); the families who snigger 'Good night' when the wireless announcer says 'good night'; women who go to a rep. theatre all the season and talk like experienced playgoers; almost everyone who tells jokes...

I think on the whole this catalogue of resentment boiled down to the usual pose, found in art and politics, of disliking fairly ordinary people.

I also kept lists of people I liked:–

Neighbours who ignore me; waitresses who can see me three hundred days a year without presuming that I can wait till the others are served; those who do not comment on the fact that it is Friday the 13th or the first day of spring or five days to Michaelmas; people who do not get sentimental or hypocritically depressed when they talk about deceased relations (I had in mind a friend of the same age who, when I asked him what his father did for a living, said: 'Well, he's been dead for three years so he can't do much, can he?' I admired him for that remark enormously).

I think most of my 'likes' were snobbery, epitomised in my 'like' of people who can see their names or the names of their friends in the paper and keep quiet about it, expressing a wish on my part to be in a position where all my friends had their names in the papers as a matter of course.

Rudeness. Not the sophisticated rudeness of cynicism, but plain, unadulterated bad manners. Thus when someone asked me if I knew where such and such a street was I would not make the usual bones of stopping and explaining but would remark 'No', or even, when I was feeling ruder than usual, 'Yes', and keep on walking. Even my wishful thinking rode along on wings of rudeness, so that I could write in my Queer Book:–

'How to make yourself unpopular –

'Next time someone is leaving your house, shout in a very loud voice "And STAY out!" and slam the door ... on meeting a friend in public, wait until he has greeted you cordially then, remarking coldly, "I don't think I've any change, my man," turn on your heel...'

And 'Things I must say immediately prior to sailing for America –

'To a hostess: "Damn you, woman, I will not have another cake. It is the foulest stuff I have ever tasted"... To an aesthete: "No, I've never even heard of Ruskin..."' (which, as a matter of fact, I hadn't until recently, and even now I don't know whether he was Russian or French, if either).

Wit. Mostly puns, elaborate things that no-one understood (such as that I didn't like Cassandra of the Daily Mirror because I thought nothing of a man who wrote Agamemnonymously)

– until everyone made up puns. Then epigrams: sarcasm is the only form of wit; the most hackneyed phrase in the world is 'hackneyed phrase'; there is more good to be got out of crying over spilt milk than in trying to put it back in the bottle. Which led to sage maxims, such as 'There's many a top hat hides an empty head'. And, of course, sarcasm, and ponderous examples of Wodehouse humour, none of which were preserved after a purge at nineteen when I rebelled against that sort of thing. 'His face was the colour of chalk. Red chalk.' I remember I thought that was extremely funny.

Power. One of the most important aspects of the Coffee stage is the sense of power that every seventeen-year-old gets – or at the least, the sense of the need for power.

This sense is usually manifested in the seventeen-year-old making himself a Big Shot at his youth club. I think it comes about for two reasons, both allied to each other. First, at seventeen one is ambitious without the remotest chance of one's ambitions being realised for some time. Second, taking a look at the Great Big World outside one gets, momentarily, stage fright. Putting this panic and one's ambitions together, one withdraws entirely into the escapist youth club life and makes it into a private world, where one is free to follow the course of one's inclinations and ambitions with confidence.

In my private world I tried to get them to run the club council on the lines of the House of Commons because I had political ambitions with visions of myself as Prime Minister.

I tried to run the club magazine like a national newspaper because I wanted to be a journalist. I even started a war, or tried to, by printing an edition of the magazine with the headline WAR! in six-inch capitals on the front cover, the entire issue devoted to denouncing someone who had crossed my path. Privately, I had elaborate daydreams about a town where only young people lived, where I was dictator, editor of several newspapers and social leader combined.

That little world of mine still exists, and there are people in it who were there when I was there, still playing, at twenty-two, their game of little worlds. I wonder if it is arrested development, or funk, or what, that keeps them there. At any rate, none of them are any very great shakes as far as personality is concerned, and they never have any wars.

A young man at seventeen is one-fifth pedant, and my pedantry came out in the shape of the English grammar.

Every day a friend called Walsh and I met for lunch, and every time one of us ended a sentence with a preposition or split an infinitive the other would tell him about it.

Sometimes we would do both in one sentence, and that would be considered highly funny.

When we got expert at this sort of thing we began to tell other people – including a minister of religion who had been educated at Oxford and Harvard – when they ended their sentences with a preposition and when they split an infinitive. If they did it too often, we cut them.

As we did not move in a particularly grammatical set, we quickly lost the few friends that Art and Politics and Coffee had left.

For this we were considered snobbish, and I wrote the following defence in my Queer Book:–

'There is no-one quite so obnoxious as a working-class snob. And there are more working-class snobs than there are aristocratic snobs. The working-class snob detests and ridicules anyone who has climbed high in the world, apes with exaggerated emphasis the man who so far forgets himself as to pronounce an aitch, imitates the well-dressed woman who hates looking round the factory as much as he hates having her look round – imitates her with a hyper-Oxford accent (I had just learnt 'hyper') heard nowhere except in the mills in those occasional orgies of contempt that have done more to foster class distinctions than any eyebrow raising in the midst of Mayfair.'

This freed me to go to whatever heights of snobbery I wanted to, which I immediately did.

I made lists of Phrases I Do Not Wish To Hear Again (He doesn't look at all like a clergyman... Churchill was a good man, but... I thought I was broadminded, but... I don't pretend to know anything about politics, but... in the book it was...) and of Entertainers Who Don't (farmyard imitators, comedians who turn patriotic, pseudo Anne Zieglers and Webster Booths, anyone capable of provoking the laughter of that loud-mouthed woman at the back...).

I revised my opinion of Shaw because I found out that he had once used the word whomsoever.

And I thought the joke about the Boston man who shot an owl because it said 'Towho' instead of 'To whom' was very funny.

Walsh and I spent most of our time making fantastic grimaces, which we always adopted on hearing a grammatical error. We were fascinated by women who knew no grammar, and longed to point out to them our entire knowledge of grammar: one, that one must not split infinitives, two, that one must not end a sentence with a preposition, three, that it is to whom.

(You must not use a preposition to end a sentence with. Ha ha. I must ask you to not split infinitives. Ha ha ha.)

Then one day we read that L.A.G. Strong or somebody once said that all the grammar he knew would fit on the back of a postage stamp, so we dropped the whole thing.

There was a period of obscurity, of going to the pictures and reading Wodehouse novels and listening to the wireless, until the Call came, and I was nineteen.

I came to be nineteen by being in the Air Force and having long discussions with a person called Alec. It was during these discussions, which took place in flat Oxfordshire lanes, in cookhouses and in hygienically designed barrack rooms, that I systematically betrayed nearly every god that I had set up at seventeen.

The Conservative Party, never a strong attraction, was

replaced by the Labour Party. I also put it to the meeting that the Communists were not to be despised either, and every day, as we sat on our beds waiting to be called out on parade, I would argue politics with the only person connected with stockbroking that I have ever met.

He would read the *Telegraph* and I would read the *Herald*. He would say the *Herald* was biased and I – claiming to have been a newspaper reporter in civvy street – would say that I knew all about the *Telegraph* and that it was corrupt.

Early on in the arguments I created a catalogue of entirely fictitious statistics and quotations, ranging from the number of unemployed men who died from starvation during the General Strike to what Mr. Churchill had said about the dockers on numerous occasions. Most of these went out of my head as soon as they were quoted, but as my opponent's memory was as short as mine I was able to put the figure of leading British Conservatives who had supported the Fascists before the war at twenty on one day and five hundred the next, without anyone noticing any difference.

Armed with my imagination, a more potent weapon than the Labour Party handbook, I was able to defend the Left against onslaught by price increase, dock strike, nationalisation loss and the increasing inefficiency of the railways until I was demobilised.

As regards patriotism, I had my attitude to that summed up in the phrase 'Shoot the King' which became, on my instigation, a camp catchword.

The Flannel Dance era came to an abrupt end. At my training camp near Bridgenorth it had had its last fling. The ex-public-schoolboy who shared my confidences there had dispersed to Southern Rhodesia fully confident that the Templenewsam Hunt did exist, and that its hounds did cross our land at Halton Moor so often as to become a nuisance.

Now, however, I was in a permanent camp where fairly interesting conversation had to be sustained for about eighteen months. The need for that landed me among Interesting People – Peter, a rather pedantic peddlar of the classics, notably Jane Austen; Alec, who talked theology; David, who understood Latin; and the stockbroker.

They were mainly public school types, one of them ex-University. The least of them lived in a semi-detached house at St. Alban's, paid for through the building society.

With these representatives of the Top Ten about me there was not much future for me as the gilded aristocrat. I could have done it on my head, but it would not have been very interesting for long. And so I became poor.

(Have I given, in those creaky paragraphs, the right impression: that I was very anxious to pose as the self-made Socialist scholar among the chosen people? I am afraid I have been reading too much Evelyn Waugh.)

Yes, and so I became poor.

I not only replaced the Estate after Halton Moor, but I inserted the word 'housing' between Moor and Estate so that no-one should be in any doubt about my background.

I indicated that we had only recently removed there from the slums.

I knocked up father again, giving him a barrow for his fruit instead of a lorry and making him bankrupt, leaving a house with orange boxes for furniture behind him when he died as a result of under-nourishment.

I denied my secondary school education, pushed my school leaving age back to 14 and claimed to have worked in a string factory, cobbler's shop, coffin makers, and as a garage hand, rent collector, newspaper boy and ice cream vendor.

I remembered how one day in my childhood my mother, when there was no money in the house for some reason, had sent one of us to the post office to cash two penny stamps so that we could have a tin of sardines for tea. I delivered this anecdote almost untouched by hand, feeling my poverty acutely because this happened to be true.

I acquired an almost homosexual love for The Miners, also for old age pensioners and other people in unfortunate circumstances.

I drew a vivid picture of my eldest brother playing the trumpet in the street for coppers after returning wounded from the First World War and being unable to find work (later worrying in case anyone realised that I couldn't possibly have a brother so old as to have fought in the First War, or wondered where he got the trumpet from anyway).

I vouchsafed for the poverty of streets of people whom I personally had observed living for a week on bread, consumed on the floors of houses in which every stick of furniture had been sold, but where the curtains had been retained for the sake of Pride.

I thought so often and for so long about poverty, searching for new and entertaining stories, that often a lump would come into my throat and I would actually believe that I was as poor as a church mouse. (Liars do that in books. It really does happen.)

In most of my anecdotes I would bring in the image of myself when young, working at home (suggesting, if not actually mentioning, an attic and a single lighted candle) on Plato or *Das Kapital*, after a hard day at the string factory.

And at length my industry was rewarded by one of my rich friends – the one from St. Alban's – prefixing an invitation to join in a discussion with the words: 'Now, *you're* a self educated man...'.

So there went Wealth and Station and the Conservative Party. Art came off rather more lightly at first.

To begin with, encouraged by the conversation of my friends, Art enjoyed a marked resuscitation.

True, I renounced Oscar Wilde – when an apparent seventeen-year-old wrote a letter to the paper suggesting that the moderns were not a patch on Oscar Wilde, I wrote such a vicious attack on him that he wrote one back, and the paper had to do a leading article on the subject to shut us up. No-one is so contemptuous of the Oscar Wilde fan as the Oscar Wilde fan recently redeemed.

I renounced him good and proper, but I fell for philosophy, collecting in a Stationery Office notebook the names of Socrates, Diogenes, Plato, Aristotle, Epicurus, Luther, Erasmus, Hobbes, Locke, Donne, Spinoza, Descartes (pronounced Day-cart), Kant and about forty others, with the intention of reading their complete output. I did, in fact, read the first few books of The Republic with great enjoyment, and even now can occasionally remember the names of Glaucon and the other fellow.

I also read De Quincey's Murder Considered as One of the Fine Arts, or part of it anyway, and I became very interested in the Every-man shelves at the bookshops. On the whole though, my taste was gradually declining (in theory, but in fact ascending) to Richard Aldington, George Orwell and Henry Williamson.

In my Queer Book I started a revised list of my fifty best books, telling myself that this time I would be more truthful, but I never got further than number nine:

1. Plato's Republic
2. Boswell's Johnson
3. Margaret Lane's biography of Edgar Wallace
4. James Hilton's Goodbye, Mr. Chips
5. A book called England, Their England
6. Odd John, by Olaf Stapledon
7. Joad's Guide to the Philosophy of Morals and Politics
8. Portrait of the Artist as a Young Dog, by Dylan Thomas
9. Week-End Wodehouse
10. —

– and as a matter of fact that was at that time quite a truthful list, except that I had entered Plato, Boswell and Joad on the strength of reading a few pages of each.

Yes, Art was on the way out. And then one day I sat down and wrote this Letter to a Highbrow in my Queer Book, and Art went for its final burton:–

'Dear Percy,

'You are not going to be attacked. Have no fear of that. But you are not going to be left alone – you are to be subjected, albeit unwillingly, to a defence of middlebrowism and, in places, the cult of the lowbrow.

'You love Shelley. You adore Marlowe. Sir William Alexander, Earl of Stirling is your god.

'But not mine. It is possible that the loss is mine; perhaps if I had the faintest inkling that Thomas Dekker was not a firm of cooked meat specialists I should be better off for it. But as I am not a highbrow, as I know very little about the accepted classics, why may I not be admitted as an aesthete?

'Consider my case.

'I like Joseph Conrad. I enjoy Somerset Maugham. I thrive on humour, and I have an appetite for almost the whole range from Mark Twain to Wodehouse. Now to you, humour in literature is probably Toby and Andrew in *Twelfth Night* or the gravediggers in Hamlet. To me it means a man pelting down the street at a rate of knots after a top hat, or a Wodehousian phrase such as 'a susurration of blighters, some male, some female'. Whose is the taste? Yours or mine?

63

'Take another aspect. You delve into the Dutch for the ideal painting. Personally I look at an advertisement for gin and plump for a George Belcher in oils of a fat man smoking Woodbines and playing the trumpet. Again, who is right?

'Who sets the standard? That is the point. And the answer is – you do, dear Percy. But why should you? *Are* you right in saying that given persons were great men and that their output represents the acme of what is good in the world's art when something like 75 per cent of the population *does not agree with you*? Jones down the road doesn't like Homer. He shifts coal for a living, and if he went in for serious reading at all he would read Gerald Kersh. But let me contend that he is as much a highbrow as you. Obviously, the high-per-cent disapprovers of classics so disapprove because they lack the education to appreciate them. But still, lacking education, they make their own classics. They fix scales for their own artistic circles, putting Paul Renin at the bottom, Ruby M. Ayres in the middle and James Hilton at the top. *Goodbye, Mr. Chips* is the poor man's *Paradise Lost*.

'You see, Percy – this is all I really want to say – we too have taste. When the whole of us together devise a system whereby we can all learn together, each as much as the other, perhaps my coalman will thumb a book of *The Iliad* as he goes his rounds. But until then he will continue to read a Western novel.

'But please! It is the very *best* in Western novels. There is taste in everything, dear Percy!

'Yours, a reluctant Philistine.'

(I didn't realise it was as bad as that. I keep telling myself, 'Ah, but they'll think you *meant* them to get the impression that you had no idea how to express yourself.')

The Coffee period lingered, but it was a perverted Coffee period. Rudeness was on the way out – I would occasionally have fits of bad manners, especially during my first few weeks as a corporal, but on the whole I was full of solicitude for my elders and betters. There was a Mrs. Wilson, I emember, and I asked after her health daily.

Cynicism, however, had taken a new turn. Poverty and Socialism had purged the snobbery out of cynicism, and I acquired a robust, sarcastic humour to replace it.

The Queer Book was littered with stuff like this:–

'If it weren't for half the people in the United States, the other half would be all of them.' (*Saturday Evening Post*)

'Well then, if you're an air gunner, where's your air gun?' (*The Isis*)

'Own up, you wash-out.' ('False Friend of the River Revellers', *Schoolgirls' Own Library* No. 42)

'A man may not marry his grandmother.' (Table of Affinities)

'Damme, you have shot my grandmother when she was not insured and when you possessed no licence to use a gun. Sir, you are no gentleman.'

'You have murdered my wife and throttled my three children Bessie, Emma and George without the slightest provocation on their part. Sir, you will hear from my solicitors.'

'He appears to have cut his throat.'

'The world would be a far better place if more politicians believed in fairies, more field marshals indulged in Morris dancing, and more solicitors lived in wigwams.'

'I'll soldier no more. You may do as you please.' (Specimen from *Manual of Military Law*).

When my nineteenth year was on its way out, it had this orgy of guffawing for a lament.

Through it all – art, politics, coffee, cynicism, rudeness, wit, power, grammar, seventeen, eighteen, nineteen – ran a vein or thread of nostalgia that is the essence of being young.

That is what it is easiest to remember, and what you do remember first in the few years afterwards.

The glint of the evening sun on the chapel windows and the scent of the flowers and the choir weaving an anthem into the evening (forgetting your abtruse theories on the existence of God).

The girl with the crinkly hair and the white blouse and the tartan skirt who used to smile back at you from three pews away, two rows down, and who was introduced to you in the vestry, and how you walked to Kirkstall Abbey together that night and for many other Sundays after (forgetting how you used to call her a bitch to your friends).

And the quarrels, and the time she danced with Johnny Cooper all night to make you jealous, and how you kissed her for the first time at the top of the street, and how the next night you left her at the bottom of the street, and she said: 'Does it make any difference which end of the street we say good night?' (forgetting how distasteful was her 'French kiss', as it was called).

And the time you threw her up for good, and she waited for you at the youth club door and said she couldn't live without you, and you smiled and took her in your arms (forgetting how you later got sick of the sight of her).

The coffee, even the coffee – sitting in a milk bar and arguing with Walsh and planning and scheming (forgetting how none of the plans ever came to anything).

The hikes, twenty of you wandering over a piece of sub-urban countryside, piling into cafes and stealing each other's apples and carefully not making any jokes about sex, and Ken Adams standing out in the middle of the road to stop the bus, and everybody piling into it and the arguments about the fares, and everybody singing (forgetting the Pyramid of Youth).

The Big Top, the summer dance hall they had on Wood-house Moor; it was a big marquee, and when you got off the tram you could hear the band playing 'Souvenirs' before you went in, and you could hear it playing 'Souvenirs' when you went away again, its tinny melancholy instilled in you for ever (forgetting that you could not dance very well, and how you once fell on the floor during the St. Bernard's Waltz).

The office where you used to work, how you would buy a shilling mince pie and a pot of coffee in the morning, and

67

how the street was scented by the tea warehouse next door (forgetting how you didn't like the work).

The winter, a new girl, and how you would walk up Harehills Lane and see her waiting under the yellow lights of the picture house, and how you walked in Roundhay Park when the frost was in the air and the day was urgent with expectancy (forgetting how the expectancy came to nothing).

The sticky back rows of the cinema, her head newly resting on your shoulder, her body warm and intimate when she took off her coat against the heat (forgetting how she said she didn't want to miss the newsreel).

Your first touch of a girl's breast, how you got nearer and nearer every night and the delicious shock of finding that there was no longer any nearer to get (forgetting how it wasn't very much, really).

The R.A.F., sitting in the N.A.A.F.I. with your friends and flirting with W.A.A.F.s, and Corporal somebody playing that record of 'So Tired' over the tannoy system every night (forgetting how you counted the days to demob, and how you said you would break the record over his head).

Leave, and how everything came back the same, the girl, the Big Top and the same tinny tune playing into you, eating right into you (forgetting nothing, only remembering the hot night, the scent of apple blossom, the trams droning at the back of you, the warm face near you and the saxophones cutting through the low murmur of voices, the bass fiddle banging out the heartbeats of those tinny years).

68

PART TWO

Here I am then, being twenty-two.

I am married and I have two good suits and I want a blazer and I drink Younger's No. 3 and I smoke forty cigarettes a day and I am a newspaper reporter and damn proud of it and I want to be a famous writer and I have daydreams about me winning the Pulitzer Prize or something with this book and them putting it in my paper saying they are proud to announce, and my sideboard isn't like other people's because I don't have symmetrical ornaments on it, only a clock and a model of a black cat, and I try to write songs and I know all about sex, and when two of my chairs turned out to have woodrot in them I went right back and told them about it and they got them seen to, and I have sold a radio play for sixty guineas and I am going round telling everybody I don't give a damn when they broadcast it now I've got my money, but really I can hardly wait, and I have just read *Life in a Putty Knife Factory* by H. Allen Smith and me and Walsh are trying to write a book which is as near like it that people won't be able to tell, and last night I saw the first performance of the *York Mystery Plays* since 15-something and I left in the interval although honestly I was enjoying it, but it was cold and I'm scared of the dark and I hope to hell there isn't another war, and there's a radio revue on the wireless and I've decided to write one myself. ('Love in horn rimmed spectacles,

    Intellectuals

      wear them

    But I can't

      bear them...'), but obviously I won't, and on my day off I clean up and make the bed and a lot of people call me Mr., and I am going to learn to drive and I have dropped my second initial, only calling myself Keith Waterhouse now instead of Keith S. Waterhouse, and my signature isn't like the late Queen Elizabeth's any more, it just says my name without any messing.

This is nobody's style but my own.

I read *Film Fun* with great enjoyment, also the *Sunday Pictorial*, and I take the *Observer* for the book ads and C.A. Lejeune, but not the *News of the World*, though I am glad to see a copy when I get hold of one, and I read *Razzle* on the sly, and I am not above pretending to be well in with Norman Evans or someone even though I might have met them only once in the course of interviewing them, and I want to go abroad and I am very fond of Smarties, also Fry's Crunchie or is it Crunchy, and I don't like anyone trying to boss me around and I get mad with them if they do and I am very proud of it, and because my name has been over one or two articles in the paper (scores really, I'm being modest) I think I'm famous, but am I hell and I get jealous when I see where Peter Ustinov is at thirty, and I back horses and I like sending office boys on errands and I have a typewriter and once a week we go shopping and then to the pictures and once a fortnight up to my mother's and every Sunday night up to her mother's for supper because that is nearer, and I go to Marshall and Snelgrove's for coffee instead of the milk bar, I suppose I should be checking the spelling of all these names, and I eat reasonable meals, once I lived on toasted teacakes, I ate eight hundred a year, and I don't want to wear glasses like I used to want to and I like people to see me with a packet of twenty Players and thank God I'm not getting called up for fifteen days G-training and Walsh thinks I make twenty quid a week, but I don't, but I told him I did.

And that (nobody's style but my own) is me being twenty-two, at this immediate moment.

Oh yes, and I fixed the gas poker up all right but I couldn't do the wireless, and I play brag but prefer to cut for half crowns and I like to have a shave straight after tea, and the reason I like people to see me with a packet of Players is because they think I'm in with a shop that gives me Players (missed that out before), and Walsh takes his hat off when he comes into my flat and I shall have to fix that lazy switch over the bed one day...

When I was a child I would never eat the round side of a piece of bread. It always had to be the half slice cut from the bottom of the loaf, so that I had a nice even oblong piece of bread.

That is something that I have carried along with me all these twenty-two years. Not in bread, but in other things. I don't mind what shape my bread is any more, in fact I rather prefer the round side − is that reaction, or just maybe I like the crust? − but I still like things to be square and even.

I like the squareness of our Baby Belling electric cooker. It is squat and white and square, and I can just sit down and look at it and look at it because it has not got all sorts of edges sticking out all over it.

I like the splash plate (what a kick you get out of knowing straight off pat that it should be called a splash plate, like getting six clues in a crossword right after each other) behind the Baby Belling. That is white, flat, oblong. The nails in it do not protrude and there is no blemish on it at all.

Once I bought a bar of chocolate and removed all the wrappings and took a bite out of it, ignoring the squares, just biting it as you would a slice of toast. It was delicious.

I love the breadboard because it is a smooth chunky sharp cornered piece of − is it deal? I don't know what they make breadboards of. (Do I sound as though I don't care, very superciliously don't care? I am afraid I am being deliberately stylish. Obviously it isn't deal.)

I wonder why I like square things. Perhaps it is because I love things to be bold. I love those hard pencils that write so boldly and blackly.

Mainly it is paper that I like all square and squat. I have a passion for paper. I have squandered pounds on reams of white quarto, not knowing what I was going to do with it – only thinking vaguely that I would fill it with writing in lovely royal blue ink, very close – but it is wonderful to sit down at a table bare of everything but a pen and a ream of shiny white paper, stacked very neatly without a single sheet jutting out anywhere. If I find a single sheet sticking out I take it out and throw it away, knowing that it would spoil the look of the pack to put it on top where it doesn't belong. I throw blank sheets away even if they have a little ink or a thumb mark on them.

I have bought fat notebooks for the same reason (I like them fat with stiff covers so that they shut tight, not flap open when a few pages have been used.) When I was making notes for this I found a thick notebook with a proper binding and a black cover, just like those housekeeping books but without any printing on. (I hate printing on books, just as when I was a child I hated having any name on my toys. Because I want to put my own names on, I suppose.)

But when I got that book I daren't write in it. I had to get a cheap threepence halfpenny notebook. I have a few books I daren't write in; one of them is a big minute book. I suppose I am keeping them for some higher purpose.

Library books I can never read without wishing they were made of blank paper. Maybe my own wish to write a book?

I do not like thin notebooks where the paper slopes down where it is stapled. Before now I have taken a ruler and a razor blade and cut the binding off one of those notebooks, cutting it right through and getting annoyed when it didn't cut even and odd wisps of paper jutted out. Then I would move the ruler back a bit and cut the wisps of paper away, keeping on cutting until I'd got it absolutely flush. Just so that I could have a nice square pack of paper. And then I wouldn't do anything with it, just fritter it away, but it was nice to have it and flick it through my fingers like a pack of cards.

I always wanted a pack of cards that were absolutely blank, and without the rounded edges. I don't know what I'd do with them, but I have always wanted a pack of blank cards, gleaming white pack, very much indeed.

I have always wanted a notebook that looked exactly like one of those fat pocket diaries, but with blank paper and no dates. Why don't they make them?

I am always disappointed when I pick up a nice-looking notebook, thick and smooth with a stiff gleaming cover, and find that it is an index book and not a notebook. I have spent hours picking up index books to find out if they were proper notebooks.

I suppose it is because I imagine them full of my writing, just as though I had a lot to write about.

I love full notebooks. When I have a few blanks in my diary I go back and fill them with all sorts of silly things – so long as they look convincing and have some flimsy excuse for being there – just because I like to see all the pages crammed tight. I have always wanted to go right through a notebook cramming every page with closely written notes on one subject, but I never have, and I suppose I never shall.

I bet all this sounds like some kind of neurosis.

I think I want to fill notebooks and love big blank books because I want to write a book.

Paper, I don't know why I love paper, maybe for the same reason.

But the moral is that when I write something I am moved far more by the sight of a fat ream of virgin paper in front of me than by whatever ideas I have in my head or whatever inspiration is in my heart. That being understood, let us get on with it.

And when I was a child I would write, along with everybody else, 'A day in the life of a lemon' or 'A day in the life of my cat'. And mine was always bestest. And when there was to be a composition written on the processes of wool shearing, it was always considered brilliant to write it as though you were the sheep.

So this is a day in the life of a twenty-two-year-old.

This morning was my day off, so I got up at half past twelve and smoked a cigarette and got a wash and shave, and then read the papers in the library.

Then I came home and we had fish and chips and then went into town, and then we came home and had some tea.

Then I read a book, it was *Men, Women and Dogs* by James Thurber and I laughed a lot and then I listened to *Twenty Questions* and then I wrote some of this.

Then we had some coffee and bread and dripping and went to bed.

Funny how all this book is me being twenty-two, and when you get right down to it all it is drinking coffee and eating bread and dripping.

Try again, different tack. What were those other essays we used to write – this time for night school: 'My job'.

My job is I am a newspaper reporter. I have been a reporter for two years, which is three years short of what I told everybody in the Air Force. And every two hours of the day I still remind myself that I am a newspaper reporter because I am very bucked about it. In my pocket is a black card marked 'National Union of Journalists' which folds up like a book, and inside it says Press in bloody great letters, also a photograph of me like in a passport, and my signature, and 'The person to whom this card is issued and whose photograph is attached hereto is a member of the National Union of Journalists'.

When I first got this card I used to whip it out at every opportunity and flash it at people. I still do when the fit takes me, but it is infra dig to tell people you are a journalist unless you have to, in fact it is infra dig to show any joy at being a journalist at all, or to write down in your Queer Book, as I did: 'I belong to a good profession, a profession begun by a few very excellent reporters, named Matthew, Mark, Luke and John. Some great reporter in Genesis told the story of the creation of the world in 400 words, and there are only 297 words in the Ten Commandments. That is great reporting' – which Quentin Reynolds wrote, and which I think is pretty good.

Only the people in the advertising department say they are reporters; reporters themselves keep quiet about it. I was very disappointed about that at first, but in fact I do find it embarrassing when people ask me what I do to say, 'I'm a reporter', but I like them to know it all the same. Except when they make jokes about you had better mind what you are saying, he'll put it in the paper, then I wish they would shut up.

I suppose all this doesn't look as though it were written by a newspaper reporter, whose books should either be Fleet Street memoirs or *Inside Whitehall*. But if I want to I can write: 'How a sixty-year-old cripple fell down three flights of stairs and lay bleeding on the floor for two days before he was found was told today at the Leeds inquest on...'

And as a matter of fact that is what I like to write. I like murders to happen, town halls to catch fire, hidden hoards to be found in the homes of dead eccentrics, because I am twenty-two.

I suppose twenty-two-year-old journalists are like twenty-two-year-olds everywhere. We boast and brag and drink beer and talk shop, and plumbers of twenty-two must do the same.

We bind a lot, why don't they do this and why don't they do that. What the hell have they made this the splash for, why the hell don't we follow this up, who the hell does he think *he* is with his golden wedding, why the hell have we filled two columns with that muck, I think old so-and-so is going off something shocking these days, don't you?

(And the forty-year-old journalists say it was ever thus, that we will learn, that it is policy to print a golden wedding. And we say to hell with policy. And they say we'll learn, we'll learn...)

And there are stories to be told: how so-and-so began an application for a job on the Daily Rag with 'Rumour tells me there is a vacancy...' and how they replied: 'Rumour, so often a fickle jade, errs again.' How so-and-so interviewed a man who claimed to have made an atom bomb in a pudding basin. How so-and-so dolled himself up in morning dress and hired a Rolls so as to get into Harewood House.

(And the forty-year-olds remember how so-and-so once interviewed a man who dared not sit down because he thought he was made of glass, and how so-and-so wrote to a woman who wanted a job: 'Dear madam, so long as I am editor of this newspaper the whoosh whoosh of a woman's skirts will never be heard in these corridors. Besides, there is not enough lavatory accommodation.' And how old so-and-so would tear the phone out of the wall when he was angry...)

And there are lines to be shot: how I got so close to Princess Margaret I heard everything she said, some smashing quotes, how the policeman thought I was one of the jurors, how I just went in and he told me the whole story.

(And the old 'uns: how he played the piano with the murderer till they came to take him away, how he disguised himself as a farm labourer and got an exclusive interview, how he hid under the table and heard the whole thing...)

And we talk about how we have not paid our union subscriptions. How funny, we talk about how we have not paid our subscriptions, just as we did in all our youth clubs long ago.

(And I suppose all this time twenty-two-year-old plumbers are talking about how they went into this room, and there was this woman just getting out of the bath, stark naked. And I suppose forty-year-old plumbers pour cold water on their dreams.)

Forty-year-old plumbers, damn them all. Me and my inferiority complex don't get along with forty-year-old plumbers. The trouble with being twenty-two is that one is eighteen years younger than a forty-year-old plumber.

I was very proud to be sent to cover the opening of the Festival of Britain, and I wrote two columns on the King at

St. Paul's Cathedral ('To the bright dignity of this mosaic of his people, a King rode to pray with all his nation...' – Edgar Wallace stuff). But there were eighteen years between me and the reporter next to me, eighteen years between me and the rude manager of a place I wanted to do a story about, eighteen years between me and the press officers. Eight or eighteen, it didn't matter, age sticks to age.

And at home, a forty-year-old secretary of a forty-year-old executive ushers in a twenty-two-year-old reporter and she says: 'There's a young man to see you.' And he puts 'do you sees' and 'do you understands' in all his explanations, and he says; 'Let me see what you write before you put it in the paper.'

And a forty-year-old man writes to the magazines to say that youth today is brash and pushing, and that it wants to be Seen and not Heard if it wants to get anywhere.

And the forty-year-old reporters go on looking down their noses at the twenty-two-year-old reporters, and the forty-year-old plumbers go on looking down their noses at the twenty-two-year-old plumbers, and the world goes round on a wobbly keel, half of it forty, half of it twenty-two.

Inside the mind of every young man of twenty-two is that youth club he joined when he was seventeen. And there his little wars and worlds and parliaments lie dormant until a forty-year-old plumber blocks his view of the world he knows now. Then out they tumble, like coloured blocks from a nursery cupboard.

I bet I have spent eight of my twenty-two years in day-dreaming, luxurious extravagant concoctions that might be escapism or wishful thinking or what, I don't know.

When I was ten my favourite daydream was to imagine myself plonked in a comfortable armchair in front of a warm fire that never needed any coal putting on. Everything I wanted was in reach. The chair had arms like tables instead of arms. On one was a lot of chocolate whirls, marzipan teacakes, mint imperials, Palm toffee, pieces of Swiss roll, Christmas cake, chocolate logs and nut cake, and on the other, bottles of lemonade and orangeade and Tizer and dandelion-and-burdock. In my hand was a good school story by Hylton Cleaver or Gunby Hadath, with a special device of wire to keep it open so that I had my hands free, and on the floor were more school stories. And my glass was automatically filled out of one of these bottles without me moving. And I would never have a yawn stuck in my throat which stops you enjoying anything.

Sometimes I would imagine myself let loose in a big storeroom full of chocolate, not in bars but in big slabs like lard, and me cutting chunks off with a sharp knife. And sometimes I would dream of having a whole nut cake all to myself.

And when I dreamed that dream I always said that when I could afford one I would buy one costing one and nine, and I did, and threw half of it away, and I have never bought one since.

What extravagant dreams they were! (But recently I pulled up an armchair in front of the fire, and on my right was a small table with brown bread sandwiches of cheese and onion, and on my left a pot of tea, and there was a packet of twenty Churchman by my side, and in my hand a Margery Allingham novel.)

Later on I would dream of a little world, an island somewhere, inhabited only by boys and girls. I was the boss of it, and we had bogies for buses and lemonade bars, and we wore uniforms of grey and I wore a high hat like a bearskin but more complicated, and I had a lot of decorations and was held in high esteem.

And later on it was a bigger world, probably the size of Lancashire, inhabited only by young people. I was the boss of it, and we had real buses this time and an underground railway and pubs and we wore civvies and I was the President, also the editor of the newspaper, also the Prime Minister, also a lot more. And we had a lot of traditions like the masons and we were a very OLD country, and when the war started we had to help out: seven thousand of us marched to war and only four of us returned. And in the victory parade we four limped up with our flag at half-mast after the Grenadiers had gone by, and they played the dead march for us and instead of cheering as they had cheered the other regiments the people took off their hats to us and stood in silence as we marched proudly by, one of us in a Bath chair, me with my arm in a sling.

82

And even now that world exists, and sometimes I creep away to it. Now I am the political leader and I run a chain of magazines and newspapers, but I am a reporter on them at the same time, and I am also a barrister arguing brilliant cases for which I get cheered, and sometimes I change from the merry laughing madcap that everybody in this little world knows to a Lord Chief Justice, and everybody takes me being serious for granted. We still have a special language in our little world (I invented it long ago, it looks like Russian), but now it is used only on ceremonial occasions, like Welsh.

Sometimes I draw plans of this little world, and sometimes I draw the front pages and the feature pages of its newspapers. First I draw the dull *Times* that is its official paper, then I draw a brighter paper – say, like the *News Chronicle* – that a rival person runs. Then I draw the *Sun-Herald* (****Fourth edition) which is my paper, a big bright sheet, which is very like the *Daily Express*. And there are catchy headlines and bright pictures with snappy captions, telling how so-and-so has resigned after a sensational meeting, how fire has ravaged a public building, how so-and-so has made grave charges against the state. And then I will produce some late news out of a hat – spy flees, premier dies, bank collapses – and change the paper round. And I will then draw my feature pages – a Giles cartoon by my friend Hill, a column by my friend Walsh, a *Daily Mirror* Cassandra column by my friend me.

(How long ago was it that I would pile dominoes on a Dinky toy and pretend it was a builder's lorry, or fill a hole in the back garden with water and wish it into an Atlantic Ocean? And you can be a teacher, but I'm the headmaster, so ner. And how long since I would edit my twelve-page youth club magazine, and dream of it being the size of the *Saturday Evening Post*?)

One day I want to be a columnist, but I do not try to be one. I sit down and make up fictitious breezy items: 'Man-of-the-moment in the snappy Soot Club is dapper, forty-ish George Johnson. Bald George can't dance, never buys a drink, is no good-looker. Yet the girls flock to him. Reason? George is the Soot Club's new resident conjuror, produces nylons from the hat instead of rabbits!'

I would like to be a radio commentator, but I do not write an application for a job on the B.B.C. I dream of out-Glendenninging Glendenning, sitting on the roof of a Fleet Street office and describing a royal procession going beneath me with remarkable pith.

I would like to know all about music, but I do not learn it. When there is nobody in I turn on the wireless and conduct the B.B.C. Variety Orchestra with a ruler.

I would like to be Al Jolson, so whenever there is one of his records on I make appropriate Al Jolson gestures and hope to God nobody comes in the room. (Once I would beat on the copper with two sticks of firewood, pretending it was a drum.)

84

I want to be the Prime Minister, and I stand in front of a mirror and make expressions that will move the public to various emotions. After I had seen the film *All the King's Men* – it is about a fanatical American politician who calls his audience hicks and gets away with it – I have often imagined myself walking on to an election platform and shouting at the audience. 'Look at you, you half-starved ninnies! What kind of a government do you want – one that keeps you in patched breeches for the rest of your life? Or do you want justice? Don't look at me – you'll get nothing out of me! I look after No. 1, same as you should do! And if you look after No. 1 you don't want me to tell you which way to vote!' And I imagine my dramatic rise to power, becoming virtual dictator, yelling abuse at my enemies but slipping shillings to children on the sly. And the films have a *This Modern Age* newsreel about me: 'Genius – or Madman?' And the *Observer* runs a Profile on me, and I move people to hysteria, like Hitler did. And I get shot, and I die, and they're sorry.

The difference between these images at twenty-two and their counterparts at seven or seventeen is that now they are kept out of sight.

Once (when I would slouch about with books in my pocket to look academic) they would come to life. Sometimes I would be the cynic, sometimes the silent brooder, sometimes the laughing, jolly, natural self that everyone imagines himself to be at heart, but which in fact is as much a pose as a seventeen-year-old being Oscar Wilde.

Once I would get on a platform and shout abuse at a youth club, once I might dare to conduct an orchestra and let my hair fall over my eyes and my sleeves roll down, if the orchestra were there. Now – because I am twenty-two – it all goes on backstage. Or most of it. Sometimes I am a reporter, sitting in shirt sleeves and very self-consciously typing abbreviated words – 'A meetg to Lds Council tt shd hv taken place today ws postponed bcse...' – and sometimes I am a drunkard, going to the Pack Horse three days running, but more often than not I am myself if – as I happen to know Jerome K. Jerome once said – such a person there be.

I have thought of running the country as a limited company, with a board of directors instead of a parliament, and I have thought of starting a whelk stall at Knaresborough.

I have thought of spending a holiday as a minstrel and then writing a book about it, and I have thought of running a mail-order business.

I have thought of a hundred and one things and I have displaced them with a hundred more. Daydreams are the lifeblood of the young man of twenty-two, but ideas are the corpuscles. The young man has the idea of writing a Western novel so he sits down and sketches the covers of a dozen Westerns which one day he will be famous for having written, and he dreams of films being made of his books, and of radio serials, and of him being made honorary sheriff of Texas. His Western novel, if it is ever started on, is certainly never finished.

86

I have written poems with the idea of writing more poems, with the idea of publishing a slim volume. And I have written popular songs:

> Lollipop Lulu,
> I love-a-love you-lu,
> Lollipop Lulu,
> How I love you!

> Bubble-gum Baby,
> I'm hoping that maybe,
> Bubble-gum Baby,
> You love-a-me too!

So help me God, that is what I wrote. And I have started on many more ('Eleven p.m., eleven p.m., we stand at the garden gate, I want to know when, I'll see you again, ti tum ti tum ti ti date...') And yes, one day I will put a lyric to that waltz of yours.

Often and often Walsh and I and Hill have sat and talked our way into the clouds, and on the castles in the air neon signs have flickered with our names, and then gone out. And we have sighed, and sat and talked again, and the neon lights have lit themselves again, bigger and brighter than before.

('Yes, that is what we'll do. Everyone will love an idea like that. And you will be the manager, and you the secretary, and you must find a hall, and you a sponsor...')

Often and often one of us had produced the definitive edition of our genius. A book, a play, a business house, a money-spinner, a garden merry with flowers. And someone has fetched a newer toy, and we have played with it, and all the rest have gone discarded.

Once we were going to write a play set in the ward of a T.B. sanatorium (*Tare Betak*, it would be called, T Tare, B Beta). Once we were going to run a Beachcomber column in the local paper. Once we were going to write a book called *A Minute of Smiths*, consisting of sixty chapters telling what happened to sixty different people called Smith, aged one to sixty, in the sixty seconds of one minute of the day.

Once we were going to put all our first chapters together in a book and call it 'First Chapters', and every chapter in the contents list would be called Chapter One. And there the beginnings of all our books – *Crime Without Years*, *Three Straws to a Cup of Coffee*, *Poet's Paces*, *Murder Most Funny* – there they would lie, all of them, in peace.

The radio programmes we have thought of would keep the B.B.C. going for three months. A revue devoted entirely to satire on the B.B.C. itself, a wireless edition of the *Radio Times*, a series of instructions on the art of arguing, a programme consisting of me and Walsh getting up and talking to each other about the first thing that came into our heads.

Whenever we heard of a good idea we would pinch it, and pretend it was our own. Thus we would read *The Iron Heel* and proceed to write *The Wooden Heel*. Thus we would see *Passport to Pimlico* and think up a film script of our own.

Thus we would steal the styles of Waugh and Wodehouse and Kenneth Grahame.

We have been going to start a cranks' club and a vaudeville theatre and a competition magazine, and we were going to run wall newspapers at tram stops, subsidised by advertisers, and we were going to start a leading article syndicate for weekly newspapers, and we were going to invent a new card game, and we were going to write a history of jazz. And one day we will gather up our sticks and stones and build our castle in the air with first and second chapters, and with a last chapter for a roof. And one day the cuckoo will build a nest.

We are the lotus eaters. And here are twenty-two years that the locust has eaten. (Youth on your Pyramid of Youth, why do you always see a bigger pyramid before you have climbed the first?)

So maybe we get no further with our new political party than a manifesto. So maybe our newspaper gets no more than a title to its name before we drop it. So maybe our books never get beyond the first chapter. Who cares? Who says that one book twenty-two chapters long is better than twenty-two chapters out of twenty-two different books?

Darling,

You haven't any need to be jealous of David, sweet, because you know that it is you I am interested in and not David, so promise me you won't be jealous of him anymore, but I am afraid I can't stop him talking to me.

I shouldn't buy yourself a halo if I were you, because even though you are trying to stop swearing for my sake I shouldn't like you to become an angel (not yet anyhow).

Well precious I haven't much more to say just now except that I liked the last part of your letter and I feel the same way about you, for when I think anything is wrong between us I just can't rest until I found out that everything is all right again, so lots of love...

Darling,

I'm glad your mother won't let you come to school on your bicycle in the summer, if only for my sake. You see, you wouldn't be able to go with me then, and I would be lonely going home without you to talk to. Hadn't you thought of that, or don't you mind going home on your own?

Are you mad at me for swearing when June Spencer's desk lid fell on my head? I couldn't help it, really darling. I do try not to swear, but when a fellow has hundreds of desks raining down on his head he has to say something.

I liked that bit in your letter about you loving me with every atom of your heart — it's poetical.

I wish I could think of some way in which to show you how much I really love you darling, but I can't. I don't think you'll ever know how absolutely mad I am about you.

Well angel, I think that's all at present. Remember I will always love you always...

The sex life of the human youth is remarkably sanguine.

Up in Crossgates, which is a suburb of Leeds, there is one of those modern public libraries made of glass, which you see mainly as diagrams in the youth sections of exhibitions. Strangely enough, the youths of the village do actually hang about there. They use it as a duck walk, which is a stretch of country reserved for the matchmaking of adolescents.

On Crossgates Library steps, then, sex raised two of its ugly heads at me and Hill. One was a candy stripe dress and a book by Monica Dickens, the other a Roundhay High School blazer and a bicycle with a little basket on the front. Hill wanted the candy stripe dress and I pretended to want the other, and we introduced ourselves.

I said my name was Trevor Austin and that I lived at 82 Templenewsam Road (which is in a residential part of Leeds) and Hill said that his name was Tony something and that he lived two doors off at No. 86. And one of the girls produced one of those letters that go the rounds, I forget what it said, but I know we had to kiss her, and she accused us of slavering, and love blossomed.

Then one day we were all getting off a tram and I fell down the steps and nearly broke the driver's arm because we were getting off at the wrong end, and he asked me for my name and address and I said Trevor Austin, 82 Templenewsam Road. And the girls wanted to know why I hadn't given him a false name and address, silly. And so of course it was never the same again.

So I got me another ugly head: one called Margaret, only we used to call her The Witch. And one day a man I knew gave me some of what he called passion pills, which were supposed to act on women as an aphrodisiac. Aphrodisiac is a word I happen to know. And I squashed up a chocolate and put this pill in it so she wouldn't know and I was going to give it to this girl on the way to Ilkley Moor mixed up in a bag of chocolates, only unfortunately I went and ate all the chocolates myself, so I could only offer her this squashed-up chocolate out of a filthy crumpled bag, and mutter up something about saving it for her. So she ate it very doubtfully, but it didn't do any good. The only effect it had on her was to produce the comment: 'It seems indecent, somehow.'

So there was another one, and we were going to get married and live in a cottage in Devon with roses round the door. And by God, she used to call me her pet lamb. And I used to tell her lies. Not ordinary lies, like sorry I couldn't meet you last night, I had to stay in, but big whoppers without any reason behind them. I made up a set of friends called Joe, Tom, Mary and someone else, also a cousin from Chesterfield, also a budgerigar which I said we had. And I used to go on in detail about this lot every night, even to what we fed the budgie on – oats, I said, good job she didn't know anything about budgies – and Tom had won a scholarship and this other chap had had his hair cut right short. And this went on for months and months and months and months and months.

The back pages of the women's weeklies are wrong, sexual intercourse before marriage is not the worst thing that can happen in the love life of youth, youth, youth.

92

The worst thing about it is the distressing amount of time wasted. Of his twenty-two years every young man has allotted three to a girl he dislikes. He has wooed her and thrown her aside, scorned her to his friends, gone back to her, chucked her once more and gone back to her again like a yo-yo, hating her even as he takes her in his arms. Yes, this time I *have* finished with her for good, the squint-eyed sod. Darling, I love you. Yes, I'm packing the cow up. Darling, I love you. God help him if he's going with *her*. Darling, I love you.

And nobody knows why. Because you're you, I suppose.

But the string of the yo-yo broke at last, and there was another girl, and we got engaged, and now we are married.

Which is more than most people are at twenty-two, so my experiences from that point on are nothing to do with the case of being twenty-two years old. So that lets *me* out.

If you have laughed at my loves as I have done, now you can laugh at my fears as one day I shall laugh at them.

Fears are jokes in the making. Whether they come true or not we laugh at them later on. (That does not look at all as though I had written it, does it?)

H. Allen Smith, in his book *Lost in the Horse Latitudes*, tells of a man who wanted to become father to an ostrich by hatching an egg. Yes, well I knew a man – this is all relevant to the subject – who actually did become father to a toad.

It appears that when a woman thinks she is going to have a baby she can send a sample of her urine to a place in

93

Edinburgh where they inject it into a toad. If the toad lays eggs within a week, the woman has had it.

That is what this man did with this woman's urine: he sent it to Edinburgh, and this toad that they injected it in laid its eggs, and these eggs presumably developed into more toads. And so this man claims he is father to a toad, if not a large family of toads.

The above is a funny story which has not been dragged in by the heels, but which has a moral to it, e.g., that It Is Funny Now But It Was Not Funny At The Time. The father of the toad laughs about it as loud as anyone, in fact much louder now that everyone knows the story. But at the time he was shaking at the knees. Like us all, he laughs now, but once he was shaking at the knees.

I am not the father of a toad, but I am the father of my troubles, and I too am shaking at the knees. One day I shall laugh at them.

I shall laugh at them as I am laughing now at the troubles I used to have. Once when I was a small boy I would go to bed at seven o'clock promptly – I mean promptly, dead on seven, not a second before or after – because I was frightened that if I did not go to bed early I would never be up on time to leave for school at twenty past eight. I would never go anywhere that would bring me back home for later than seven o'clock, not even to the auntie at Horsforth where there would be cream horns for tea and a strange cupboard with toy trains. And once I was in bed I would refuse to

94

open my eyes even when my brother came back from Filey with a brand new telescope, because I thought that once you opened your eyes you were back where you started from in the matter of going to sleep.

And when I was older and delivering morning newspapers (ho yes, I was a paper boy, that is how all the biographies begin), I would be scared stiff of making mistakes. On the last street of my round, the street that brought me back to the shop again, I should have two papers – a *Daily Mail* for No. 98 and a *News Chronicle* for 142. If there was ever a mistake, it always showed itself here. And my heart was always in my mouth when I turned into that last street. What if there were two *Daily Mails* and no *News Chronicle*? Or what if there was one *News Chronicle* and no *Daily Mail*? Or even worse, three papers altogether, so that I had to take one back to the shop?

And sometimes I would think about death, and how I did not want to die, and I would work out how much longer I had to live and console myself by saying that I had six-sevenths of my life to live. And then I would sweat in case I ever got buried alive.

And one summer in my days of dirty knees I heard about a girl who was turned out of a fish shop for having lice crawling over her. And for months I was haunted by visions of lice; I would look for them and follow up every tickle. One day I found some heat midges on my knee. I cried all the way home and scrubbed my legs till they bled.

And often I would think about grown-up people, wondering how they managed to keep themselves, and I would be terrified that when I grew up I should not be able to manage my affairs in the big world and I would starve in it.

And every day I would come home from school wondering whether anything had been found out about me, and all day long and all night long I would have my worries reeling round my head, so many that on the rare occasions when I had nothing to worry about I would be jubilant, or when I had just one worry on my mind I would tell myself: 'Directly you have paid back the threepence you borrowed from the milk money, you will have nothing to worry about at all. You won't have any worries on your mind.' But somehow it was never for long. There was always something to worry about. Schooldays are the happiest days of your life.

Now I am twenty-two, laughing at the fears I had yesterday, shaking at the knees at the fears I have today.

I am afraid that I might have T.B. I am afraid even as I write this because I remind myself of it. I smoke forty cigarettes a day and I cough like hell. Every time I spit I look to see if there is blood in it. I stuff handkerchiefs down my throat to see if they come up stained red. Every medical book I get hold of I look up T.B. Ever since St. Leger Day last year I have had a yawn stuck in my throat, I am short of breath. I get people to reassure me that it is only with smoking. When I get pains round where I think my lungs are I am relieved when I find it is only a spot on my back. I will not see a doctor, I do not even have a doctor, because I am too damn lazy. But I am frightened that if I ever did turn out to have T.B. I should spend my days regretting that I did not see a doctor while there was still time.

I am also afraid that I am going to get cancer with smoking, as I read in the paper today that Doctor somebody says you can; yet I will not give up smoking.

. I am also afraid of my four dreams. I have these four dreams regularly. In one I am driving a car (I can't drive in real life) and skidding dangerously round corners and sometimes, I think, crashing. In another I have either just murdered someone or am just on my way to Borstal, and I am telling myself that I haven't stuck to my record of not murdering people – or not going to Borstal – after all. In another there is a dread, dark building with a dread, dark staircase with a dread, dark Thing at the top of it, something I am terrified of, yet I insist on going up this staircase. And in the last dream it is not really a dream at all. I simply wake up and there is someone in the room, and I cannot move, I cannot move a limb, I cannot speak, I cannot scream. When I really wake up I find that I only dreamt of waking up. And those are my four dreams. I do not know what they mean. But I am afraid of them.

I am also afraid of torture. I lay awake thinking of horrible tortures – the rack, the thumbscrew, the iron maiden – and I think of that Hogarth picture and people gouging out other people's eyes and all sorts of unspeakable things.

I cannot get them out of my mind. I sweat. (At first I wrote: 'I lay awake thinking of horrible things that I am too afraid of to bring to mind so that I might write them down.' That is not true – I can bring them to mind all right. But in George Orwell's *Nineteen Eighty-Four* I read that They, whoever They are, always know what torture you fear most. I didn't want Them to know what torture I fear most. That shows you how scared I am.)

I am also afraid that there is going to be another war. I am afraid of there being another war not because of any high ideal, but because I do not want to go back into the Air Force: first because I did not like the Air Force when I was in it, and the Air Force did not like me, and second because I shall probably get shot. I do not want to get shot. That sounds exactly like the new heroism, the kind you find in novels or films about the new patriotism: 'Christ! I didn't want to be a soldier. I didn't want to die for my country. None of us did. We all wanted to stay back home and play with the kids. But you've got to look at it this way. Maybe if we don't come out and fight maybe we won't be *able* to play. Maybe there won't *be* any kids.' That sort of thing. But I do not want to die because maybe I want to live.

There is a man round our way who made a pact with his brother shortly before going off to get himself killed in Korea. This pact was a vengeance pact, by which the second brother followed the first and avenged his death. He followed him to Korea, where he was immediately posted missing.

The press called him a hero. So, I believe, did General MacArthur. I call him a silly ass. There is another man round our way who got a medal for standing on a rock firing a Bren gun at the enemy. I call him a silly ass too.

Now to all third persons – everyone to whom that statement is reported – that is a shocking thing to say. It is blasphemy.

But to all second persons – the people to whom it is directly said – it is a perfectly normal thing to say. People are saying it to each other every day. All my friends agree that both these national heroes are silly asses. They say it themselves: 'They are silly asses.'

Then who *makes* heroes of the heroes? Not the public, not my public. My public calls them silly asses. And my public is a big public. Because my friends have friends who have friends who have friends who have friends who have friends, and between them they take in the world. Who makes the heroes?

I have a friend who calls himself a Thinking Man, and he says it is propaganda on the part of the Capitalists who are agin the Communists, also it is unconscious propaganda on the part of the people who have heard the propaganda in the first place and swallowed it and repeated it.

Personally I do not think it is anything of the sort. I think it is all a mistake. I think that everyone thinks that everyone else thinks that heroes are heroes, and acts accordingly. I think that newspapers imagine their readers want heroes to worship and cater to suit them. I think that a few silly old women carry this hero worship far and wide to people who do not like to argue the point. I think that heroism is a national myth. Myth says that Montgomery is a hero. I have never heard a good word said about him. Myth and the *London Gazette* say that the man who stands upon a rock firing a Bren gun is a hero. Everybody says he is a hero. But everybody says he is a silly ass. Heroism is a myth.

Now someone is going to talk about ignorant youth, brash youth, seen and not heard ... men fought and died ... freedom to have foolish opinions ... if youth of yesterday had thought like that ... jackboot ... learn wisdom with the years ... Dunkirk ... Battle of Britain...

Yes, all right, but as a matter of fact I and my friends do not believe that there was any heroism about the Battle of Britain, or Dunkirk, or El Alamein or anywhere else. We are sorry, but we do not believe it. Similarly, in spite of all the evidence put before us by Harry Price and others, we do not believe in ghosts. The facts might be overwhelming, but we do not believe them.

And since you mention it, I and they believe that the youth of yesterday *did* think like that. Suppose I had the chance to stand on a rock and fire off a Bren gun. Would I have done it? Yes, as a matter of fact, I would. But not for the supposed reason that I wanted to save my country and my comrades. For my reason, and I think for the reason that anybody stands on rocks and fires Bren guns, you have to go back to being seventeen. You have to go back to the sentiments you think you have got but which you haven't really – flag waving, lump-in-the-throat patriotism, visions of medals, visions of oneself on the films, visions of glowing citations. I could stand on a rock and think I was a patriot, just as I could stand on a hill and think I was a cowboy when I was four.

And if you want to bet on it, the generation that is twenty-two years old now, with me in it, could go off and fight a battle pretending to be patriots and people would believe us, just as they believed the armies who fought the war for them.

I am also afraid of the dark. Often I go away and I have to sleep in strange rooms in strange hotels. I lie on my pillow and stare into the darkness, learning the geography of my unfamiliar room, switching on the light to confirm that what looks like a man is a wardrobe and that what looks like a wardrobe is not a man. Once I spent a night alone in a deserted youth hostel that had been a barn. I was driven half frantic by the weird noises – creak, creak, shuffle – and the shapes that leaned back in the dark when I turned my head. I would recognise footsteps with that sickening 'Gonk' that is the heart's last beat before it stops in fear, and identify them as wind in the beams with that sigh, unheaved, that brings relief and leaves the body shaking.

How many years is it since I would lie restlessly in bed, waiting for the friendly footsteps on the stairs that would bring a brother to bed and scare the night off into its own darkness? How many years since the bogey man called last?

It cannot be very long ago. It must be yesterday, it is so recent. And if it was yesterday then it will be tomorrow too, for childhood is as near to twenty-two as that.

Yesterday, was it, that we toured the playground catching people out with the latest repartee?

'*Have you gorram?*'

'*What?*'

'*Spots on your borram!*'

But it was yesterday, when we were twenty-two, that we sat on a barrack bed and chanted to each other:

'*To the woods!*'

'*No, no, not the woods!*'

'*To the woods!*'

'*But I'm only thirteen!*'

'*I'm not superstitious!*'

Was it yesterday that we were reprimanded for lewdness as we sat near the window, looking out with pretended nonchalance, but singing:

'Whistle while you work,

Mussolini is a twirp,

He wipes his bum

On chewing gum

And sticks it on his shirt...?'

But it was yesterday (and we were twenty-two yesterday) that we sang in the office, as though we were singing the latest popular song:

'Ever since you met my daughter,
She's had trouble passing water...'

Yesterday when we were juniors we would look with envy at the seniors, whose badge of office was the woodwork apron they wore on the day they had the woodwork lesson. They would come to school wearing their aprons tied round their waists, but rolled up inconspicuously beneath their jackets. Then yesterday when we were seniors we wore our woodwork aprons modestly beneath our jackets, but we made sure to keep our jackets open so that everyone could see.

But yesterday – when we were twenty-two – wasn't that the day when we walked into a pub as carelessly as you please and ordered a bitter as though we had been ordering bitters all our lives? And was not our stance – expertly propping against a familiar bar, expertly toying with a familiar glass – part of the same game of nonchalance played by a boy in a new woodwork apron?

Yesterday we would long for all those essential items to a boy's compendium of boyhood – new skates, a bicycle, a gun, a fishing rod, a pair of football boots.

And yesterday we got them, and they had changed to cuff links, armbands, a watch, a signet ring, a fountain pen, a camera, a typewriter. And still we covet them, as − if we ever got it − we coveted our bicycle. Armbands and bicycles are confirmations that we children need. A boy with a bicycle is officially a boy; a boy with armbands is officially a man.

Yesterday we were made prefects because we were old enough to accept the responsibility of authority. We cuffed the first junior we saw because we loved our right to responsibility more than the responsibility itself.

Yesterday we were made voters because we were old enough to accept the honour of citizenship. We voted for the first name that came into our heads because we loved our right to citizenship more than citizenship itself.

Yesterday we would go home from school and fabricate a story about the headmaster's car skidding on the ice and turning upside down, and how he was trapped inside and the ambulance came and the headmaster jumped out unhurt.

And yesterday we would tell of what we said to the boss, and what he said, and what we said right back, just like that.

I have reached out too often with my hand
Seeking the rusty ice ripple of the brook,
Looking for smooth pebbles in the sand.

Yesterday as I straggled, prone,
Reaching for heaven, my fingers touched
Warm water and a jagged stone.

I wrote that yesterday. I do not remember how old I was. I meant, if I meant anything, that I had sought my pleasures too often and for too long for them to be pleasures any longer. It was only yesterday that I would be afraid of taking all my toys out of the cupboard at once in case I tired of them and wanted to go out, and the time taken to put them away would be so long that melancholy, that awful young melancholy, would set in as I scurried about stuffing lead animals into the cupboard. But I did not write a poem about that.

Are there many sour grapes in the garden of youth? It was not yesterday, it was today that I woke up in one of those strange rooms in one of those strange hotels. The sun was shining over the marketplace outside, and the town was busy with men pushing barrows and setting up stalls. Downstairs there was the smell of frying, there was the prospect of a good cigarette after a good breakfast, of a stroll to the paper shop for the *Daily Express*, of coffee later at the bun shop, of a bus ride home and no more nights in strange hotels. When I look through the window of one of these strange rooms on a bright morning, my inside turns to liquid with an absurd and frothy delight. That is the reason for my being twenty-two. And in this bath of shallow exultation is to be found – after you have searched the tub where the Union Jacks are starching, the sink where the latest ideals are steeping, the stream where the poets are paddling – there in this bubble bath of buoyancy the soul of youth, perhaps of all humanity, is to be found scrubbing its silly back.

PART THREE

Like I said, here I am being twenty-two. And being twenty-two is like I said it was. Yes, I have had the reaction you get when you're twenty-one, when you're sick to death of everything you ever thought about. And yes, I put the shutters up on my mind. And yes, yes, I took them down again and sorted out my ideas, and some I kept and some I threw away and some I got in fresh, and here I am.

I find myself in a definitely earthy world.

My world, I mean. It is rather a shock for me to discover what an earthy world it is. I have dabbled so long in ideals and the general salvation of man that it is a bit of a blow to find that I am more inclined to settle down with a Carter Dickson mystery novel than to dig out the latest report on prison reform. I had always suspected it, but I never believed it.

If this book were dated – you know the sort of thing, *Paris, June–November*, it would read *Leeds, April–June 29* and *Leeds,*

September 1 to whatever date I finish it. That is because since June 29 till the present day, September 1, I have been learning card tricks with a view to becoming a competent amateur magician.

I wouldn't have believed that if I hadn't been there myself. I should have thought that I would diligently plod through my book, putting one profound thought on top of another until I reached the end.

And in my leisure moments (I would have said) I would have one serious discussion after another. Making enquiries, I find that I do indeed have serious talks with a serious friend about, say, the shortcomings of magistrates' courts, leading up to the shortcomings of justice, leading up to justice as a broad general principle, leading up to the shortcomings of all broad general principles, leading up (unfortunately) to taking a card, any card, in the pack.

And in case this looks like a humorous essay about the time father took up golf, I have to give other examples.

Before I thought that I would become a magician I had a little puzzle to occupy my mind. It is a little puzzle which, I have since discovered (but to no avail, for when the mood takes me I still try to solve it), has in fact no solution. It is this:–

.   .   .

The first dot is the waterworks, the second is the gasworks and the third is the electricity department. Now then:–

.   .   .

That first dot is a house that wants water, gas and electricity laying on, the second dot is also a house that wants gas, water and electricity laying on, and so is the third. But the occupants of these houses are not very friendly with each other, so they will not allow the pipelines going to other houses to cross their pipelines nor to go through their own particular house. So each supply has to go from each department to each house separately. In other words, you've got to join each of the three top dots to each of the three bottom dots without any of the lines crossing or joining.

I explain that puzzle at length because I have been into it at length. I bet I have spent a total six months of my life just trying to do that puzzle on bits of paper.

And what I am getting at is that I have broken off more political essays – no I haven't, I never wrote a political essay, I was too busy doing that damn puzzle – all right then, I have broken off more short stories, more articles, interrupted more thoughts, just to do that silly little puzzle, joining three dots to three other dots.

So you see what I mean about my earthy world. My five years of arty coat-turning has left me with several card tricks and a puzzle to do with six dots.

And yet I seem to be on a good thing. It seems to me that my views on the world are more mature when they come second to 'Find the Lady' than when they were at top heat in a kind of mental pressure cooker. What I've got to say about the negro problem, if I have anything to say about the negro problem, seems to have more of the measured tread of reason about it when it follows on a trick with a tumbler and a coin than if I was bubbling over with the negro problem and little else.

I don't mean to say that I think I'm mature. Though maturity (as I have been trying to shove in all evening) is probably the ability to mix godliness with the gardening. I mean to say that I am more mature than in the days when my ideals – my shabby, false and hollow ideals, but ideals just the same – ruled my living. I mean to say that the ideals I have left, the ones that come after card tricks and puzzles with dots, are real ideals. Or nearly all. I have some unreal ideals, some false values, that I know to be unreal and false, but I like them unreal and false and I believe in their falseness, if that means anything. I like my twenty-two-year-old justice even if it is cockeyed, and I stick to at least some of my guns even if they don't shoot straight. Perhaps that is why I am not mature just yet, because I haven't the heart to put all my beliefs under the microscope and certify them twenty-two carat gold or throw them out as brass, one or the other. Brass and gold still look the same colour to me.

My ideas on politics when I was seventeen and nineteen look pretty daft, but you ought to see what I just wrote now, when I was writing down what I think of politics now I am twenty-two.

What I wrote is this: To hell with it. That is what I wrote.

Now, that's not a very nice thing to say, is it? It is not very constructive, to begin with.

But I am afraid I mean it. To hell with it. To hell with the Labour Party, the Liberal Party, the Conservative Party and the Communist Party.

To hell with Mr. Attlee, Mr. Clement Davies, Mr. Churchill and Mr. Phil Piratin, who I don't think is their equivalent in Communism but is the only name I can think of at the moment.

To hell with the Keep Left Group and the Keep Right Group.

To hell – and a special hell for them – with World Government, Social Credit, Common Wealth, World Union, the World Movement for World Federal Government, and the Liaison Committee of World Citizenship Associations. A special hell, because I've had a bellyfull.

And that is a warning to all horn-rimmed pamphlet-heads with an interest in getting me to come to the aid of their particular party.

I think I have been spoiled for politics by a surfeit of theories. And that must be some surfeit, because theories are what young men are made of.

Looking back I see that it had to happen. And probably thousands more young men will never cast a serious vote in an election because they are off their politics for the same reason as I am.

Last time we saw the political me I was nineteen, wasn't I, and – as it were – red raw. Half Communist to the half-baked gills. Socialist to a fault.

Being nineteen, of course, I couldn't let the Labour Party alone once I had accepted it into my circle. I had to keep probing it.

And being of a black-is-black, white-is-white turn of mind, as often as not I found it wanting. I took my disturbed thoughts to superior friends well up in the political world and they smiled cynically and said that of course, it was obvious that the government was just an extension of the American radio network, or that of course, it was obvious that the government was priming the people for a war, or that of course, the government was still the mouthpiece of the bosses.

By the time I was twenty-one I was satisfied that the Labour Government was a collection of people who had been leftist in their time, but were now fairly Tory in their views. The Conservatives I had long ago ceased to consider seriously. The Liberals I thought of as a bunch of hair-splitting pedants.

Thus I renounced the basic political parties as being something out of a child's drawing book and took up with the idealist movements that lurk like malignant diseases to strike a young man in his prime.

Prompted by my clever friends, literature poured in from every quarter of the globe. I still have some of it wrapped up in a parcel and at this date I can publish a fairly entertaining selection from my postbag:–

The People's International Movement, founded by a Mrs. Gregory, writes: 'The people must realise that in this age of science, past and present laws throughout the world are a menace to humanity. To counteract the building up of armed forces, an UNARMED ARMY, consisting of men and women, should be enrolled. It should be sent from each country to every other country, there to meet and discuss their country's needs.'

Some movement tied up with the future of a paper called Sanctuary Quarterly writes to me with the following demands: 'The abolition of hydrogen and atom bombs, education of the people from fear, selfishness, greed and lust; race and religious discrimination to end; prevention of hoarding of wealth, money and land by a few; not more than five and a half hours work per day, for five days per week; social security for sick and aged; free medical and dental care; expendable money, that is, all money and credits shall expire at end of each year; no man to have a salary more than five times that of another, that is, no salary less than five thousand dollars a year, none more than twenty-five thousand; freedom of worship or non-worship, the non-church member to be as highly regarded and respected as the churchgoer, provided he is moral and conducts himself in orderly ways; for de-linquents, fair and just court trials by jury drawn from the people, punishment to consist of confinement for proper education and rehabilitation. The price of *Sanctuary Quarterly* is one dollar per year.'

An organisation called NAMY sends me these few lines: 'Money is not a commodity. It is merely a gambling symbol and has no relation to proper living. Nature is man's real capital. NAMY teaches the real economy of Nature's gifts.'

Sorry, Single Tax organisation, I can only quote a little of the lot you sent me: 'The value of land obtains, inheres, in the population; that is, the value of land is created by the population. Where there is no population there is no value in land; where there is no population there is no governmental expense. Therefore, shall not the value in land be utilised to defray the expense of government? If not, why not? Do away with taxes in the single tax.'

And here is a bright little message from the League of Freedom, who say: 'We maintain that all the Great Powers, including Russia, are engaged in a furious armaments race, a mad rush to mutual destruction. This lunacy must be stopped. It can be stopped only by the PEOPLES of all countries…'

The Christian Animals' Welfare Society writes: 'We recognise that the different movements in Humanitarianism are all moving, some consciously, some unconsciously, towards unity, and the aim of this society is to bring together Christianity and Animals' Welfare…'

Never mind, Bernard Dybwad Brochmann ('I am hated by all in authority because they plainly see that I am a danger to The

Established System') – *you just go on running your sociological journal in Norwegian just the same.*

The All Age Pension movement asks me to sign this form: 'We the undersigned ask the World Government to levy a uniform individual income tax and use the money to pay a uniform pension to every individual man, woman and child from birth until death.'

Finally, to close my corner this month, here is a letter explaining the aims of the Co-operative Capitalism organisation: 'Every hour anyone works is called a work-credit hour and becomes a unit measure of interest in the total equity of the co-op. It also is counted as the measuring device to determine who is to receive time off duty when seasonal, cyclical or technological unemployment occurs...'

To hell with it. I have a hundred and forty more societies and movements and leagues where they came from, but leave them be. They have done their share. They have got me out of goodness for good.

If ever I did start a movement it would be a movement for the abolition of all movements. There ought to be no welfare organisation with loftier intentions than the People's Dispensary for Sick Animals.

Some of my clever friends, God bless them, talk graphically (by which I mean like graphs) about the numbers of man-hours wasted in the present unsatisfactory system. That is mainly what I have got against their own silly little societies. Nobody cares if George Jones says the earth is flat. What matters is when George Jones gets a whole mob of people spending eight hours a week trying to get other people to spend eight hours a week trying to get still more people to spend eight hours a week in the interests of flat-earthing.

It won't do. These ten-a-penny cloud clubs are grabbing too many of our bright young things. Half my friends have sacrificed their energy and enthusiasm on one of the altars of idealism at the expense of good jobs, or at any rate good prospects. (Funny, you never get a career man who knows Esperanto.) True, half of them are in ideals because that's the only place where they can be big shots anyway – but the other half are in because the first half dragged them in.

When I argued the point in a pub with Walsh the other night he (World Citizen number something or other) said well, someone's got to start these things. *Socialism* was just a bespectacled ideal when Keir Hardie stepped in. No it wasn't, I said, Keir Hardie stepped in when the time was ripe to step in, and he stepped in on the exhausted bodies of screaming idealists who had worn themselves out long before the battle started. Just as the Keir Hardie of World Government, when he comes, will build his headquarters on the graves of the Single Tax organisation and the All Age Pension movement.

I sometimes try to imagine all the youthful energy that is tucked away in the thousands of world-saving organisations. I try to see the lot of it centred in one big office – Salvation Ltd. – with its own commercial travellers and its own P.R.O. and its own advertising slogans ('Goodness is good for you'). I try to see whether it would be any use, anyway. But in the middle of my thinking, along comes someone out of a pamphlet box and says: 'Let us try to co-ordinate all the organisations which exist for the general welfare of the community.' And the Christian Animals' Welfare Society recognises that the different movements in humanitarianism are all moving, some consciously, some unconsciously, towards unity.

Then I give up. I've given up, now. I hope the Labour Party or someone like it does very well for the country, but I don't take any active interest. The offshoots of Socialism reached out and strangled me.

Just before I went down I had a pipedream idealist scheme of my own. It was called the Reform Party. I wrote a manifesto on eight half-quarto sheets consisting entirely of sub-headings. At the risk of becoming a bore, I give them in full:–

Law reform – abolition of capital punishment, institution of degrees of murder, abolition of prisons in favour of rehabilitation hospitals, Borstal reform, abolition of certain indictable offences – e.g, sodomy – replacing them by the term 'social offences' and treating them as such, abolition of blood sports.

Education reform – civic and political knowledge to be taught in schools, leaving age to be raised as high as possible, abolition of free schools, discouragement of Catholic intimidation, compulsory adult education where necessary,

Penguinisation of all books and pictures, subsidies for all the arts, prohibition of propaganda in newspapers other than those clearly labelled Tory, Liberal etc., rational censorship laws and complete abolition of the present system of censorship, prohibition of anonymous letters and articles in the Press, stringent advertising laws, teaching of basic world citizenship in schools, including Esperanto.

Church reform – re-parishing of redundant churches, education by University degrees in psychology, social services and theology for ministers of all denominations, prevention by law of all cant and intimidation by the church, discouragement of narrow-mindedness.

Electoral reform – institution of proportional representation, compulsory voting, civic knowledge test for all voters, by-election in the case of a member being appointed Speaker, abolition of the House of Lords, substituted by a second house of intellectuals and reformists, an intellectual vote.

Capital reform – nationalisation of all basic and necessary industries, toleration of free enterprise in offshoots of basic industries and in non-essential works up to a prescribed limit of profit, abolition of inheritances outside a prescribed limit of capital, abolition of hereditary titles and estates, social credit system for men of proved ability to build up their own businesses or careers within the limits prescribed above, industrial courts for trade disputes, encouragement of co-operative systems in free enterprise.

War reform – abolition of conscription as being useless, institution of a civil army with civil rights, ignoring the cant that military discipline is necessary in war, take part in the arms race if necessary, on account of an arms race never led to war, be isolationist in so far as taking sides in other people's wars is concerned.

Peace reform – trade only with other reformist countries and Socialist countries wherever possible, build up around the reformist countries a commonwealth which will gradually exclude the rest of the Capitalist world; encourage reformist propaganda abroad.

After this reasonably ideal state of affairs is reached, it said on my eighth page, I would scrap Parliament and replace it by a bench of judges, so that anyone who offended against any of these points would be tried just as if he had been caught pinching lead, and if he had anything against the state he would come up and argue his right to disenfranchise himself the same way as he could get a divorce.

That state of affairs is what I once wanted to see, when I used to worry about things like that, and frankly (I am only twenty-two) it is what I should like to see now.

You are now laughing. Hee hee, you are saying, his list is lengthier than that *Sanctuary Quarterly* thing, it has more dreams in it than Mrs. Gregory's People's International Movement.

Yes. But I kept my dreams to eight half-quarto sheets of paper.

To hell, also, with Art.

That is very seventeenish of me – but I am afraid it is being seventeen what done it. I suppose I never got over the bout of cultural indigestion that followed a surfeit of Oscar Wilde and Co.

My general attitude at twenty-two towards Art is that Sir Alfred Munnings doesn't like Picasso, so what, Picasso doesn't like Sir Alfred Munnings, so what, poets can't make a living, so what, and Trollope has enjoyed a marked revival, so what.

It is only two years ago since I brought my taste in painting down from the *Mona Lisa* (where it never was anyway) to a George Belcher painting of a man playing the trumpet. Now it has had another devaluation and my favourite pictures will be found among the covers of John Bull, in Ronald Searle drawings and in the Lilliput doodles of a person called Danny Colman who does a funny picture of sadism where this hangman is playing swings with the body of this fellow hanging from the gallows.

It is two years ago since I forsook Ezra Pound (whom I had never accepted) for Chesterton's *The Donkey*. At the moment the following is my favourite poem:

Uncle Tom and Auntie Mabel
Fainted at the breakfast table;
Children heed this awful warning –
Never have it in the morning.

It is two years ago since I closed my unopened copy of *The Iliad* and took up the *Portrait of the Artist as a Young Dog*, by

Dylan Thomas. Now my bookshelves have a green look from contact with too many mystery Penguins.

If I made lists of my fifty best books now, which I do not, not even beginning them like when I was nineteen, it would probably run like this:–

1. *Life in a Putty Knife Factory*, by H. Allen Smith
2. *Hangman's Handbook*, an exceedingly clever book putting the case against capital punishment in a very clever way
3. *The Confessions of an Innkeeper*, by John Fothergill
4. *The Marx Brothers*, by Kyle Crichton
5. *Delight*, by J. B. Priestley
6. *Shooting an Elephant*, by George Orwell
7. *Vile Bodies*, by Evelyn Waugh
8. Mussolini's *Autobiography*

And so on.

And I find it pays well. I find that I can hold a better discussion with my friends on *The Cruel Sea*, which we have both read, than on *The Odyssey*, which neither of us have read, though I have a Penguin copy and no doubt so have they.

Somewhere the Oscar Wilde period must still exist, for it is as inevitable as toothache. But the seventeen-year-olds who yearn for the green carnation or whatever it is may be pleased to know that at twenty-two they will be wearing not a green carnation, but the badge of the local bop club – and they will be just as pleased with it.

For this generation of twenty-two has its own aesthetic movement, without using either word – without, some of it, knowing what the first word means anyway.

It is a movement in which rapture over Aubrey Beardsley and Max Beerbohm caricatures is replaced by an enthusiasm for the cartoons of David Langdon, Ronald Searle, Peter Arno; where Oscar Wilde himself is replaced by S.J. Perelman; where whatever music they used to have in those days (told you I didn't know anything about it) is replaced by 'Too Young' and 'I Tawt I Taw a Purdy Tat'; where the *Yellow Book* is replaced by *Lilliput*; where the epigram is replaced by the latest from Groucho Marx.

It is a very funny movement, but there are a lot of people in it. Someone ought to write a book.

I suppose when you come to think about it people of twenty-two are very humorous people. They have an enormous capacity for silly remarks and an enormous appetite for silly books and silly cartoons and Danny Kaye and Michael Bentine.

By the time they are thirty, of course, they may have settled down to the Book of the Month, along with the rest of the world. Maybe I can tell you that better eight years from now.

And that is all there is about Art. Like I said, the hell with it.

Then there's God.

I have thought a good deal about God. Most people of

my generation have, though there are other generations who count the empty pews (seventeen rows, thirty-six to a row, then there's the Lady Chapel, call it eight hundred) and say we haven't. Actually it doesn't matter whether we have or not, as it transpires, because having thought of God a lot of us have decided that we didn't need to, anyway. (That's put in more as a smart thought than anything, and this whole thing is becoming irreverent. Start again.)

I was wandering round the graveyard of St. Mary's Church, Middleton, four days ago, when a thought clouted me and sent me spinning.

It was this: *You will be dead within fifty years.* Every year is one year nearer. Every year you celebrate the anniversary of your death. One day you will peter out for ever. Repeat, for ever. And the next day – possibly even the same day; no, not the same day, you *will* be famous – the next day the world will go on knitting as though you had never happened.

It was no longer funny that I had once cracked: 'I believe in death after life.'

It started me thinking about God. And the way I think about God these days is this:–

'I don't believe in you, but if you're listening, don't you take any notice. After all, you can't blame me, can you?'

Then I tell myself that I don't believe in heaven – and if heaven's listening, I'm still joking – and wonder what you feel like when you're seventy and you know you've got perhaps another ten years on earth, God's earth or whose?

And then I wonder what I wondered in my cynic-ridden teens, whether God is a backcloth to hide the black nothingness of death (I stick to the teenish phrase) or an insurance policy for the meek in taste. A hackneyed thought that leads me to a hackneyed path of thinking, trodden by me and millions in our search for God, or rather our search for a fairly reasonable excuse not to believe in God, just in case there is one.

I first met religion when I was a choirboy at that unremembered age when one does become a choirboy, and having read about how Tom Brown in *Tom Brown's Schooldays* knelt down to say his prayers in face of criticism, I knelt down to say mine in face of no criticism whatever, and felt one hell of a prig.

My prayers took the form of please God let the war end and don't let our Kenneth be killed and don't let Tiger have any more kittens and that woman, don't let her go hungry, and don't let me have nits in my hair and don't let any rabbits get caught in gin-traps and so on. I added to the inventory every night and at length it got so long I couldn't possibly remember it. Then I tried to say the *Lord's Prayer*, and found to my horror that I had forgotten it. There was an interlude in which I resisted the strong temptation to worship a small ivory elephant which stood on my bedroom mantelpiece, and my religious grounding was complete.

That was all from God until I was about twenty. Then, seeing myself as one of those thinking men you read about,

I began to think. And when a young man begins to think about God he becomes an atheist.

I did it in a very obtruse way. My first kick against God was to be in the very odd position of believing in Him but disliking Him intensely. (How self-conscious I am over that capital H.) The way I reasoned it was that if God existed he ought to be ashamed of Himself for all the misery there was in the world, and whether parsons said it wasn't His fault or not, He ought to stop it off. If I made a machine, I argued, and someone else threw a spanner in the works, I wouldn't sit back and say 'It's him what done it' and let the machine go to pot. I should mend it. So, etc. etc.

But I am afraid I held that theory more because I thought it was rather an original one than because I believed in it.

Then I read somewhere, 'Christ was crucified by respectable citizens in their right minds.' I liked that. It set me going again. I added my bit to it: 'I agree that "Jesus wept" is probably the most beautiful phrase in the Bible. But if it had ever been written "Jesus laughed", I'm not so sure that I wouldn't have preferred that.'

I liked that too. And I produced version two of theory one, i.e., even if God does exist, which I very much doubt, why should I worship Him?

That was more of a thought than a theory. There was a time when I really wanted to know the answer to that one, when I tried seriously to find one. No-one could give it to me. I had long arguments about it with a theological student, who told me that I was a good boy at heart but just independent, that's all. 'And', he said, 'you'd like to smuggle good into the world, while God stands by, a watching customs official.'

That pleased me and I wrote it down in my Queer Book, but it didn't get me anywhere. The nearest I ever got to knowing why one should worship God was a decision I reached after reading Cassandra's column in the Daily Mirror, where he quoted a version of the Lord's Prayer as it had been put about by a pastor in the Solomon Islands. It went like this:—

> Papa belong me fella, stop on top;
> Name belong You he tabu,
> Pidgin belong You he come down along ground
>   same on top.
> Give me fella kai-kai enough along today,
> Forget him sin belong me fella, all same me fella
>   forget sin belong all together.
> No let him fella long something no good, but help
>   him me fella long something good.
> Pidgin belong you, Big Fella Strong belong You, Light
>   belong You, altogether.
> Amen.

That moved me profoundly for about half a day. I thought many kind thoughts about this pastor and his simple flock, and for the moment I believed in God, and loved God.

But later I decided that what I had believed in and what I had loved was the simplicity and beauty that made this pidgin prayer a good thing. I decided that one might love many things for the same reason, and I decided that God was simply the common denominator of them all; that, in fact, all the good things in the world became much better if you issued them in a uniform edition under the title God.

And, I supposed at the time that was a fairly good reason why people should worship God.

It looked all right on paper, that one, but it never seemed to work out right. I found my churchmen a spineless crowd, and I still do. I could not see these kneeling natterers getting any more joy out of that Solomon Islands prayer than out of the latest sidesmen's rota.

I rallied twice to the churches, once when my theological friend tried to put some blood in their anaemic steeples by quoting at me those robust preachers – of the seventeenth century, was it? – who broadcast sermons with such meaty titles as 'A shove from behind for heavy-arsed Christians'. And once when I visited a Unitarian church, where they let you keep some ideas of your own.

But I found at length that my ideas, even the ones they let me keep, weren't at all Unitarian. My dislike of the church was too deep, to begin with. I don't know how I came to hate the church, but I did. Maybe it was in listening to the litany of incompetence in hospitals and injustice at pensions tribunals that is the folklore of the housing estates.

In these orgies of righteousness there is always, sooner or later, mention of the meanness of some particular cleric, how the Rev. So-and-so went for an offering to a house where there was only one loaf of bread and how he took that loaf; how the Rev. Such-and-such went to someone's mother to try and persuade her to make him a Roman Catholic – what she said to him and what he said to her and what she said right back again. Or maybe it was the seedy cautiousness of the parsons I had met. There was a time when I liked hearty parsons, radio parsons and parsons who talked broadly about sex and who drank beer, but even they did not put the answer to the question that was in my heart – why can't the churches do some bloody good? – and some of them I began to hate too, and others to like only as good blokes gone wrong.

It is probably oh so silly of me to say that the churches are no good. Only this week I did the church notes for my paper, and there was St. Someone or Other appealing for Ovaltine for the old people. But somehow I cannot forgive a church for having a vicarage restoration fund when there are so many things for it to do with its £2,000 target, so many other things for it to hold its bring-and-buy sales for.

Now I make jokes about the church, and because God is their God, I make jokes about Him too, or listen to my friends' jokes anyway. I laugh when a friend with a beard claims of it: 'It's genuine Jesus Christ.' I laugh when another friend claims to keep a holy cow in his garden. I laugh when another friend yet does a ceremonial dance round a ring of black candles in Middleton Woods. It is a guilty laugh, but it is a laugh all the same.

I suppose it is a guilty laugh because there might be some God or part of God who is too big for churches, a Mark II God, and if that is so then that might be the God I worship. I once wrote a poem about it, I cannot remember whether for effect or because I meant it:–

There is no altar in the wood,
No candlestick upon the yew,
Nor paupers' pew,
No halo round the bud.

The drovers' road about the moor
Runs well without a sister aisle;
The beaten stile
Rejects a transept door.

And where the branches of a tree
Spread out, there is no cross.
The tethered horse
Has never bent the knee.

But when the organ blare has ceased
And when the church's doors are sealed,
Upon the field
God stands – without a priest.

I think I must have meant it, for there was another one:

I will not hear the hymn,
The canting prayer,
Nor tolerate
The dog-collared soothsayer...

– and that one I never did finish, because it was a bitter one, all destructive. The first one was more constructive and it probably expresses what I felt at the time. Not in what it says – that I believed in God so long as He kept out of church – but in the feeling it awoke in me, and still awakes in me, the same feeling that I had when I read 'Papa belong me fella', the feeling of love for a God who should be called goodness.

If that God does not exist, if it is just an emotional state the same as a Lassie picture, if it is all done by mirrors, Idon't know where my faith lies. I suppose we must all have a faith. Maybe mine lies in a corner of my heart I have not seen yet. Or maybe I have written it down somewhere in these pages and never even noticed it.

Next to godliness comes, not cleanliness, but cruelty. I cannot think of God without thinking of all the misery there is in God's world. And the thoughts of misery stay with me long after the thoughts of God have gone.

I think most people of twenty-two with any imagination at all are tortured from time to time with thoughts of man's inhumanity to everything he can lay his hands on. When I was a child I saw someone plucking the legs off a living fly.

I couldn't keep the thought of it out of my mind for weeks. And ever since I have collected instances of cruelty the way other people collect stamps. Or rather, they have collected me. Somehow they come to me, trailing their guts behind them, like beef to a butcher's.

Someone tells me about a pig that fell out of a lorry on to its head. It is supposed to be a funny story. But I think poor pig, I think, poor, poor pig. And I think about the pig for three days. Then someone else tells me about a sea bird, I do not know its name, that had its beak deformed so that it could not hunt for fish, and that is supposed to be a touching story full of pathos. But it touches me too hard and I think poor bird, poor bird, and the visions of its sufferings haunt me and push sleep away.

It occurs to me that this turning of pain into pathos is just a natty way of disguising unpleasant facts. Disney does it. His startled fawns run in a panic through blazing woods and they lose their mothers. But we do not feel for them. We only feel a pretty-pretty pity that makes us shed crocodile tears. Only the children feel it in their hearts. And they are told, to comfort them: 'It's only a picture.'

But it isn't only a picture. It is the half of a very murky truth. Fawns are not only losing their mothers, they are losing in them in particularly gruesome ways. We know it, we cannot do anything about it, we embalm their bodies in celluloid and offer them up at the Odeon to quiet our aching hearts.

When I have had an unusually heavy week, when these tales of gore are two a penny (a sheep on Ambleside has had its teats slashed off, a boy pushed a cat down a drainpipe in Quarry Hill, children hung a dog from a tree and set fire to it), I sometimes think quite seriously that I shall eventually go mad. I think of all the instances of cruelty before me and then I think, these are only a fraction of all the horrible things that are going on, just three drops in an ocean of blood. I hear about a dog that falls down a mineshaft in Cornwall and I think, how many more dogs will fall down that mineshaft and how many have fallen down before. And how many have fallen down other mineshafts and never been heard about, never got into the papers. And all the dogs that have never fallen down mineshafts, but have met even worse calamities like being kicked day after day by a cruel owner, week after week, month after month. And all the animals that are not dogs but have met worse calamities still, all the old bears that are led about on chains and made to dance, all the lions kept in square small cages, all the cows slit open by savages and the mouse that swam three hours in a bucket and the pig that had its back legs paralysed and when it ran it trailed its legs behind it and scraped the skin off. All the animals in the world, that is. All the animals in the world.

Somehow it is not the same with people. I could think for ever about people and I would never feel exactly the same helpless, hopeless need to cry out or creep quietly away and swallow a full bottle of aspirins. It is not the same with people. People can look after themselves. Sometimes I wonder how that old man I saw selling matches today will fare tonight, what will he have for supper, where will he sleep. Sometimes I wonder whether the young blind man I met, who said that nobody loved him and that he wished he was dead and that his mother hated him – I wonder whether he will be happy now. But when I hear of a gull dropping into the sea from exhaustion my heart leaves people and goes out to it.

I wish I could be conscious that cruelty is going on without hearing about it. I wish I knew how nature makes her subjects suffer and how nature's subjects make the subjects beneath them suffer without seeing it or hearing it for myself. The other day a man asked me to sign an anti-vivisection petition. I signed it, and he said, do you want some literature about vivisection, some pictures perhaps. I told him no, I don't want to know anything about vivisection, nothing more than I know already, but if my name is any use to you on that paper you can have it. I want to sign papers that say away with gin traps, away with blood sports, but I do not want anyone to go into details about why the papers should be signed.

That is the way I would rather have it. I want to know that vivisection exists because I know it ought to prick at my conscience, but I don't want to know how it exists because that would prick at my soul. That is why I skimp those articles in the *Sunday Pictorial* where they tell you how a fox's tail was pulled straight out of its body. I do not think anyone with a genuine regard for creatures can read stuff like that for very long without going insane.

I am afraid that a lot of people have the wrong idea about cruelty. Their interest lies with the tormentor more frequently than with the tormentee. When I saw in the paper about children cutting up live kittens with a knife, people were talking about the children, what devils they were, they ought to have the birch, their parents ought to be in prison, look at the way they must have been brought up, what will they be in a few years from now.

I was thinking about the kittens. I think everyone ought to be thinking about the kittens. I think the whole nasty bloody world would be a nicer bloody world if everyone was thinking about the kittens.

There is a craze on at the moment of writing for child cruelty cases. I do not feel a great deal of emotion about them because like I said, people can look after themselves. But I see people reading a column about how little Johnny was beaten with a copper-stick, turn to page five to see how he was put in the cold water tub for wetting the bed. I see them reading it in anger.

I do not see why anyone with any pretensions to kindness should read a report on child cruelty in anger. They are obviously not thinking of the child. They are thinking of the horrible father or the horrible mother. And as far as they know or seem to care, after the case is over the child might have gone to hell. The only topic of conversation the next day is that the parents only got fined, they ought to have gone to jail the swine.

How can you feel sympathy for the kittens and anger for the children at the same time? The two emotions are as far from each other as the two poles.

If everyone thought about the beastliness of the hunt rather than the beastliness of the huntsmen there would probably be no hunt at all eventually. I do not suppose I really believe that. But it is the way I comfort myself when I think about cruelty, as I often do think about cruelty. Everyone is out of step but me, I think. If everyone else would think the way I do, then may be we could get something done. Until then it must go on hurting us, all the animals in the world and all the people who feel for them.

I dare not look forward to the day when everyone else does think the way I do. I know that probably I would still do nothing. When I stay awake and think of birds starving in the snow, that knowledge comes sometimes and nags at me still more. I comfort myself by saying that even if all the people in the world banded together to stop cows being tormented by small boys and rats being thrown into pieces of whirring machinery, even if they did stop it all off there would still be nature, the great tormentor, feeding her little ones to her big ones, feeding her big ones to bigger ones still. Nature the bully would be dropping her dogs down

134

mineshafts, letting her pigs fall on their heads, deforming the beaks of her sea birds. When I think of that I feel that there is very little hope for anything.

Clap hands, here comes justice.

People don't matter, I said. People can look after themselves, I said. It's not the same with people, I said. Well it isn't.

Faced with a dying dog a young man of twenty-two feels nothing but a sickening sympathy. He feels it worse because there is nothing he can do. But faced with a dying man, not a run-over man but a starving man or a hounded-by-people man or a man due for hanging, then he feels different. It's not the same with people. Only other people are to blame for their predicament. And there's a lot that a young man of twenty-two can do about them. Who dat called this Jew a four-by-two? Take that! Who dat called this negro a dirty nigger? Take that! Who dat wouldn't give this ex-convict a job? Take that! Youth the crusader is here, armed with the spanner he couldn't manage to throw in Mother Nature's works.

But why was it never who dat cut these kittens in half, take that, who dat hung this dog from a tree and burnt it, take that? Probably because there only individual humans were to blame, because there was enough anger being shoved on to them anyway from people who felt more about them than they did about the kittens. But when there is downtrodden humanity at stake then a system is to blame. And youth is a devil for systems.

A young man with a world to put right does one of two things. He does like I wrote about, joins an organisation and tries to get peace on earth by club vote and up-to-date subscriptions. Or he does as I do, which is to have small arguments in pubs and to refuse piously, on occasion, to listen to any jokes about Jews.

I have been dabbling in justice, or what passes for justice among young people, ever since I set off five years ago on the way to being twenty-two. What passes for justice, we had better get it straight as this is what we are talking about, is as follows: (a) anti-Semitism, (b) prejudice against negroes, (c) victimisation of the criminal classes by sending them to jail, (d) victimisation of the criminal classes by not trusting them with the safe keys after they come out of jail, (e) imprisonment of sodomites.

I have no doubt at all that those five cases are taken up by the great majority of earnest young people because they are the most picturesque lot for a zealot for justice to work out his enthusiasm on. Other oppressed-minority problems, such as votes for idiots and the welfare of distressed gentlewomen, are left for the mature.

The fact that his bundle of oppression has a certain amount of glamour attached to it does not, in fairness, mean that the young man does not feel deeply about it. When I was at school I once said to a boy who had just refused to lend me twopence: 'Don't be a stingy Jew.' Then I remembered his name was Jacobs. I felt deeply for him, all right. Shortly after he started calling himself Jackson. I do not think it was because of me.

But I have never called anyone a stingy Jew since. Not because I ever took a vow not to, but because shortly after that I found myself, I do not quite know how it came about, appointed a defender of Semitism. I found myself denouncing anti-Jewish talk wherever I found it. I refused to listen to jokes about Jews, even perfectly harmless jokes where it just happened that the bloke was called Ikey. I turned off the wireless when Issy Bonn was broadcasting, not quite realising he was privileged. I rounded warmly on people who said: 'Oh, some of my best friends are Jews, but...' I produced figures, even where none existed, against people who claimed that there were no Jewish roadmenders, that the Jews never joined the Army, that they never went down the mines, that Jewish businessmen controlled half the factories in Leeds. Ho no they don't, I said, and even if they did, which they don't, what about it? Haven't the Jews got as much right to run businesses as we have, I said. What if the Jews went round complaining that the gentiles ran half the factories in Leeds, I said. Anyway, I said, the Jews are as good as we are. But to people who got that crack in first I would declare just as hotly that it was a damn silly statement to make, because to say that *they* were as good as *we*, you see, implied that they were different which they were not, but the same – I mean that was the whole point, they were just people like us. You see.

I was a very silly boy. I didn't know what I was talking about. But I meant well.

At the same time I was plugging the lot of the negro. Whilst letting it pass when ex-servicemen called Italians 'wops', I could not let it pass when they called negroes 'wogs'. I was deeply shocked to hear that one of my friends had been court-martialled for kicking a negro in the face, at the same time calling him a dirty black nigger. He got off, I think. I was genuinely disturbed by Southern American mock-trials of negroes accused of rape. I could not do much about it beyond sign a petition that probably never reached where it was supposed to be sent and no-one takes any notice of petitions anyway.

Jews and negroes were always the loud pedals of my judicial organ. I soft-pedalled it a bit for convicts and sodomites.

For the convicts I would put in a word only, as a rule, when someone was urging more jail for them or down with model prisons. I would tear up readers'-letter pages that contained demands for the re-introduction of the cat, and I would warm to the man who trusted an ex-convict with a responsible job and the custody of the cash box.

Sodomites have received the scantiest portion of my zeal for justice. I have defended them always, but usually, I am afraid, on theoretical grounds. I have always argued that as there is no law against homosexualism in women there should be none for homosexualism in men; that, in fact, it was jealous women who first brought the law into being, in ancient Greece or somewhere. Whether that is true or not, I don't know. I once knew a homosexual and persuaded him not to be one any more, I think I did, anyway. And I have always said loudly that putting them in prison will only make them worse, they want special treatment and the judge doesn't know what he's talking about when he says they'll get it in jail. That is all I have done for the sodomites.

I am sorry to say that all my one-man crusade has been carried on, desultory though it may be anyhow, in absolute ignorance of the true facts or even any facts at all. What I know about my subjects is as follows:–

1. Contrary to popular belief, the Government was not practically controlled by Jews in the year that Reynold's News printed an article saying there were no Jews at all in the Government. I forget the date, unfortunately.
2. Negroes are just as intelligent as we are because look at Paul Robeson.
3. Prisoners use knives and forks made of a soft metal so that they cannot do any harm with them.
4. Sodomy was encouraged in Greek schools at one time or another.

I suppose that is a shocking background for anyone who is carrying on a part-time campaign in defence of minorities. Probably the organisations who look after that sort of thing, if there are any, would not care to have me associated with their names.

Probably the Jews don't care to be bracketed with sodomites nor the negroes with the convicts when it comes to a point, anyway. Probably I have done a great deal more harm than good.

But I don't think I have. There are many young men and women who are carrying the same torch as I have carried, and they are carrying it with the same blissful ignorance of what it is all about. I think that when hot-headed youth talks rhetorical nonsense on a cause near his heart he is doing some good, however. I don't know how, but I think he is. If he can get a forty-year-old to argue with him he must be doing at least as much good as Mrs. Gregory's People's International Movement. There is something to be said for hot-headed youth when it comes to flaws in systems. He cannot mend the hole in the wall himself, but he can shout till the cows come home, and when the cows walk through that hole on their way home then someone else will notice it.

Personally, I am not so hot-headed as I was, over my oppressed pals at any rate. My enthusiasm came to a head a couple of years ago when I saw those films that were going around in defence of Jews and negroes – you know, Pinky, Gentleman's Agreement and that. I planned newspaper serials pointing out how Jews, negroes and ex-convicts (but not sodomites) were being shat on, as the phrase goes, in this country. No newspaper was interested in my idea of posing as a Jew, negro and ex-convict (but not sodomite) respectively in order to get first-hand material for these articles – principally, I think, because it had already been done with marked success in one of these films, which is where I got the idea.

My interest waned a bit after that and I stopped having arguments with learned friends. But I still have arguments in pubs, though not so frequently, and I still stick up as ever for my minorities when the need arises.

Sometimes I lapse, as I have always lapsed, and as everyone lapses from time to time. Someone starts attacking the Jews and I sit back and say yes, hm, yes. I am ashamed of it afterwards, I am ashamed of it now, I don't know why I say it, but I do. Yes, hm, I agree with them. Sometimes I add bits of my own. It is not, I swear, that in my heart I agree with what they say. I think it is just the perverse need of a twenty-two-year-old to be pleasant on occasion – pleasant to people I mean, like suddenly talking about football when I couldn't care less about football. Perhaps it isn't being pleasant, perhaps it's just being like everyone else for a change.

And when someone tells me how in their mess in Abyssinia they had in regimental orders the notice 'With effect from today, His Royal Highness the Duke of —— (naming an Abyssinian nobleman) will not be referred to as That Black Bastard' then I laugh. And I still laugh, because I still think it is funny. I suppose I should sacrifice my enjoyment of the joke to my principles, which are that he isn't a black bastard at all.

And sometimes when I am in court reporting I have

watched someone go down for fourteen years without a flinch – without a flinch from me, I mean – only being glad that it is good copy. Sometimes I think, I should talk about justice, I should say who dat called this negro a dirty nigger, take that, who dat called this Jew a four-by-two, take that. Sometimes I think I ought to just shut up.

And then I think, if people of twenty-two didn't cry into the wilderness, who would?

Damn. I missed a bit out of that one. Where there's that line about when people say 'Some of my best friends are Jews, but...' I should have brought in that quotation I have from an American Rabbi who once said: 'Many of my best Jews are friends, but...' Damn.

I've missed all sorts of things like that out. There's that chapter on religion. I once heard a vicar sum up the Ten Commandments as: 'Thou shalt not do this and thou shalt not do that, and if thou dost thou wilt get it in the neck.' That should have gone in. Oh, it should, shouldn't it?

And politics, politics. Oh, hell, somewhere I've got a quotation from some author or other, he was famous I know, who said that he would be alarmed if his son were not a Communist at twenty-two, but more alarmed still if he were still a Communist at some other age, I forget what. I should have dug it up and put it in. And those chapters on when I was a child. There were some observations to be made on box kites, and oh so many things about when I was a child.

I am not inclined to revise it. I am more inclined to think ten, eleven, twelve pages more and then I've finished; more inclined to think ah, I have written a book, at last I have written a book, than to go back looking for mistakes.

I wonder what it will look like in print, bound in a nice stiff cover with a yellow dust jacket, or what colour will the jacket be, and will there be a photograph of me, and will they advertise it? And will there be reviews and will the Sunday Pictorial attack it, and will a clippings agency send me cuttings, and will I see it in Smith's bookshop, perhaps a whole pyramid of my book (like the Pyramid of Youth, remember?) because he's a local man, you see. And who will see it and what will they think of it? Will Mr. Exley see it and Miss Crosby, they both taught me English, what will they say? And Walsh and Ingham and Hill and Alec and Peter Webley and Mr. Clarke and Mr. Price and Brian Parkes – will it ever reach Brian Parkes out in East Africa? They send you six copies, don't they, what shall I do with them? Shall we keep one or two, two I think, one to read and lend and one to keep and they will go between the plaster dog bookends. And who will the other four go to? We must make a list and eliminate people.

I am sorry, only you see I have never written a book before. The manuscript lies in front of me, the original bound in a green spiral binder, the carbon copy in a manilla spring-back folder. They look good, they are an inch thick of paper each. Remember how I like thick squat piles of paper, there are two of them now and how I love them. How many copies will it sell? What will they charge for it? Shall I have to write the blurb or will they? (Sorry, so sorry, I have never written a book before.)

I suppose I ought to be humble and consider all the faults there are in my book. No I don't, I don't suppose any such damn thing. I don't feel humble even though I do know there are faults in it because I don't care because I have written a book.

I suppose I should have said a lot more, to begin with. People will say coo, is this all he has to offer, and it isn't. After I wrote my chapter on religion I sat down and had a long discussion on religion with Ingham and what we said was far more interesting than my chapter. I should have rewritten it, but I was too damn lazy. And another thing, what I said about cruelty, does that fit in the book or should I have written it like the other chapters? And is there too much rhetoric and too much dragging jingles in by the heels? I'm fond of both you see. And I shouldn't be surprised if I haven't contradicted myself from page to page and tried to make out that I'm a mature old man and tried to sound as though I knew a lot while declaring that I knew nothing, and I shouldn't be surprised if someone says the damn book should never have been written.

I don't care. It is written now and even though the pub-lished book to come is a delightful new experience to be tasted, the written book, the work, has gone. I have already forgotten a lot of what I said and I couldn't read my own book now, not if you paid me to.

Come to think of it, I don't suppose I could have even written it, not if I'd started now. On and off, more off than on, I've taken six months over the job and of course, being twenty-two I've changed a lot of my ideas since I started. Some of the ideas I wrote down six months ago I don't have now, and some of the ideas I have now in connection with chapters I wrote six months ago don't appear in said chapters because I didn't have them then.

But then, in four months I shall be twenty-three. And already I can tell that twenty-three is a vastly different experience to being twenty-two. You know how you can get a preview of your coming year – like popping into a pub when you're seventeen and a half to see what it'll be like when you reach drinking age, only in this case it's to do with thoughts and things like that – well, I think I have an idea what twenty-three is going to be like. I think the start of twenty-three will be the conclusion of the journey I started when I was seventeen, I think the end of twenty-two will be the dumping ground for all the rant and rubbish I have picked up in those five years, or most of it anyway, and that I will go into twenty-three with my money's-worth of experience. Or will I? I say I think I will, but maybe really I just hope I will.

When I am twenty-three, and technically that is going to mean the moment this book is shipped off to the publisher, there are all sorts of things I am going to do. I am going to write another book and another radio play and some short stories and some articles, and in general I am going to earn one hell of a lot of lolly in 1952. Of course I have written a book and a radio play already, but this will be different; it will be doing it as a matter of course, always one book or play on the go like people who always have the kettle on the gas.

I will do more things instead of thinking about doing them, I can feel that coming. The other day I saw a mouse-race at a fair, I thought it cruel and I was going to ring the R.S.P.C.A., but I never got round to it. A year ago I would have said that someone ought to tell the R.S.P.C.A., this year I nearly told the R.S.P.C.A. myself, next year I am pretty sure that I will tell the R.S.P.C.A.

I will be less precocious, I can feel that coming too. Already I have practically stopped arguing with my elders; I just listen to what they have to say and mostly ignore it. Next year maybe I will listen and take some more notice, a bit more notice anyway.

I will modify my views. My enthusiasm has already waned in respect of several things I felt intensely about and I always put it down to the enthusiasm burning itself out, like a piece of red-hot coal. But perhaps it is because some of my ideas are really caricatures of themselves and I am starting to boggle at some of them. And perhaps next year I will fill in the detail and knock out some of the bold lines,

KEITH WATERHOUSE

and perhaps that will be a good thing, or perhaps it won't. I am still sufficiently a revolutionary to hope it won't.

Probably these New Year resolutions sound intensely silly to everybody who is twenty-three. It may be that it isn't anything like I think it is going to be. Like when you think of heaven, I can only guess. I am guessing from the symptoms, but perhaps I have got the symptoms without having the measles. Never mind.

Things are changing, though, no-one can deny that to me. Remember the Big Top I told you about, the summer dance hall where you could hear the band playing 'Souvenirs' as soon as you got off the tram? They don't have the Big Top any more, but I often walk past where it used to be. And sometimes I have stopped and in some nostalgic dimension I have heard those tinny trumpets playing 'Souvenirs'. That is because I have particularly wanted to hear them, because they reminded me of seventeen, the beginning of these five remarkable years.

'Souvenirs' has been getting fainter lately. I have stood on the Big Top site and listened hard before I heard it. That is because I am leaving seventeen behind, because soon I shall be twenty-three and if I remember anything I will remember being twenty-two.

I suppose at some time in the future they will come back, those tinny trumpets. I will remember them down the years, and I will remember seventeen and twenty-two and twenty-three altogether as the youthful days.

147

Only first they must disappear completely. One day soon I shall stop where the Big Top used to be, and I shall listen, and I shall not hear anything except the tramcars droning past.

April–October 1951

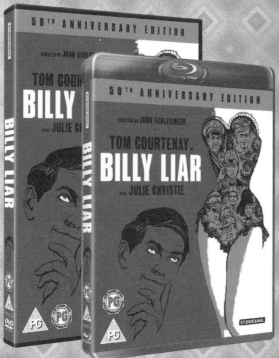